CRITIQUE OF PURE VERBIAGE

Ronald Englefield

CRITIQUE
OF PURE VERBIAGE

Essays On Abuses

of Language in Literary,

Religious, and Philosophical Writings

RONALD ENGLEFIELD

Edited by G. A. Wells and D. R. Oppenheimer

Open Court
La Salle, Illinois

OPEN COURT and the above logo are registered in the U.S. Patent and Trademark Office.

Library of Congress Cataloging-in-Publication Data

Englefield, F. R. H.
    Critique of pure verbiage: essays on abuses of language in literary, religious, and philosophical writings/Ronald Englefield; edited by G. A. Wells and D. R. Oppenheimer.
      p. cm.
    Includes bibliographical references.
    ISBN 0-8126-9107-5.—ISBN 0-8126-9108-3 (pbk.)
    1. Language and languages. I. Wells, George Albert, 1926–
II. Oppenheimer, D. R. (David Richard) III. Title.
P106.E54   1990
400—dc20   90-34128
                                       CIP

CONTENTS

ABOUT THE AUTHOR

Frederick Ronald Hastings Englefield was born in 1891, the second son of a London solicitor. From childhood onwards, from his own account, he was "a bit of a bookworm". Family life (there were two sisters and two brothers) was cheerful and affectionate, though not very eventful. Ronald was sent to Mill Hill School in North London, where he won a scholarship to St. John's College, Cambridge, in 1909. Here he studied modern languages, and came away with a first class degree in French and German. After teaching for a short time at a private school at Bowdon in Cheshire, he enlisted in the army on the outbreak of war. He was posted to France, where he survived four months of trench warfare, after which he was transferred to an officers' training camp in Scotland. In 1916 he was posted to Salonika, where he remained until the end of the war, taking part in the Bulgarian campaign of 1918. There is a piece of paper which came to light after his death, dated 1st March 1919, and signed by Winston S. Churchill, who was Secretary of State for War at that time. It says that Lieutenant F. R. H. Englefield, of the Hampshire Regiment, was mentioned in a Dispatch from General Sir A. F. Milne, dated 1st November 1918, for gallant and distinguished services in the field.

The year 1919 was a watershed in Englefield's life. His wartime diaries contain philosophical musings, comments on books he had been reading, and a good deal of verse, but very little about military matters. In 1919 he underwent an intellectual and emotional upheaval, which seems to have been at least partially stirred up by reading a now almost forgotten novel by H. G. Wells, *The Research Magnificent*. He made a solemn, almost religious, vow to devote the rest of his life to the study of human thought and human behaviour. Fifty years later, having in the meantime acquired an astonishing stock of learning in history, psychology, philosophy, mathematics and natural science, and having written several millions of words on his chosen subjects, he was still pursuing the goals which he had set himself in 1919.

Between 1920 and 1952 he taught French and German, at first in Bowdon and later at the Stationers' Company's School in North London. Out of school hours, he presided over a very popular Natural History Society, in a laboratory equipped largely at his own expense. From late evening up to the small hours, having corrected the boys' exercise books, he was busy with his own reading and writing. There was little or no time left for the usual social pursuits. He never married, and lived from 1926 onwards in the company of his mother and two sisters, in the later years reduced to one sister, who survived him.

Until the 1950s he had taken no steps towards getting his ideas into print. By 1961 he had produced a manuscript of some half-million words, entitled *Language and Thought*. This contained material drawn from several earlier projects, all more or less unfinished. The letter of refusal from the publisher to whom it was sent was respectful, almost encouraging in tone, but tactfully pointed out the difficulty of publishing a work of this length by an unknown author, without the active support of men with established reputations. Further attempts met with further rebuffs.

Over the last few years of his life, his health and his eyesight were failing. He was old, tired, and discouraged, but went on working and writing, showing an undiminished skill in detecting, dissecting, and exposing pretentious humbug. Much of the material included in the present volume was written in this final period of his active life. Sadly, only one article (of 1974)—an attack on the modern 'science' of Linguistics—found its way into print during his lifetime. The rest of the publications listed on p. x (apart from the poems of 1917) are posthumous. They include two books, both consisting of edited and abridged extracts from the *magnum opus* on *Language and Thought*.

In January 1975, after a short illness, Ronald Englefield's heart stopped beating.

ENGLEFIELD'S PUBLICATIONS

1917:   *Songs of Defiance* by Frederick Ronald. London: Erskine Macdonald.

1974:   'Linguistics: Science or Pseudo-science?' *Trivium*, 9, 1–18 (Cardiff: University of Wales Press).

1975:   'The Origins, Functions and Development of Poetry', *Trivium*, 10, 62–73 (University of Wales Press).

1977:   'The Vices of Literary Criticism', *Question* 10, 18–29 (Pemberton, London).

   Language: Its Origin and Relation to Thought (edited by G. A. Wells and D. R. Oppenheimer) Elek/Pemberton, London; Scribner, New York.

1978:   'J. G. Frazer and the Psychology of Magic', *Question* 11, 15–24 (Pemberton, London).

1979:   'Kant as Defender of the Faith in Nineteenth-century England', *Question*, 12, 16–27 (Pemberton, London).

1980:   'The Nature of Thinking', *Question* 13, 23–44 (Pemberton, London).

1981:   'Appearance and Reality', *New Humanist*, 97, no. 1, 13–17 (Pemberton, London).

1982:   'John Robinson and Others Reconsidered', *New Humanist*, 98, no. 1, 17–19.

1984:   'The Pretensions of Style', *New Humanist*, 99, no. 2, 17–18.

1985:   'Uses and Abuses of Language', *New Humanist*, 100, no. 1, 16–17.

   The Mind at Work and Play (edited by G. A. Wells and D. R. Oppenheimer) Prometheus, Buffalo.

The editors gratefully acknowledge permission to use in the present volume material from the four articles listed above for *New Humanist*.

EDITORS' INTRODUCTION

We, the compilers of this book, share the good fortune of having been pupils (in the one case during the 1920s, in the other some twenty years later) of the late Ronald Englefield. For the past twenty years we have also been collaborators in an effort to bring his work to the notice of the reading public.

It is thought by some that we live in an age addicted, as no other age has been, to the reading and applauding of pretentious nonsense. We are unable to judge whether this is so; but it cannot be denied that there is a lot of it about. Our motives in trying to propagate the Englefield approach are no doubt mixed; but they include the desire to meet the flow of portentous blather with his combination of clarity, common sense, and erudition.

Englefield's views on the nature (and hence on the legitimate uses) of language are to be found in his first (1977) book; and his account of the thinking process, which in human beings is so intimately bound up with the use of language, can be found in his second (1985) book. In these he has a good deal to say about mistaken theories of the nature of language; he includes strictures on a number of well-known writers on the subject—among them Russell, Ayer, and Chomsky—and gives some examples of the application of language to the purposes of obfuscation and myth-making. The present work continues Englefield's onslaught on the enemies of clear thinking and purveyors of hocus-pocus; but we, the editors, feel the need to explain, in the first place, the intellectual base from which the attack is launched. Obviously, we cannot summarise in a few paragraphs the arguments put forward in the two earlier books; but we can at least attempt to give an outline of his position.

In the first place, he did not see humankind as a uniquely privileged species of animal; he rejected the idea that the existence of language was proof of a fundamental difference between man and the rest of the animal kingdom. Language, he held, was a human invention, like the wheel, and its existence did not require a mystical explanation. Its origin was to be found, not in the largely instinctive cries, clicks, and other noises used by animals in general, but in the use of self-explanatory gestures, designed to promote co-operation in a social animal not much cleverer than a modern chimpanzee. In his book on language, Englefield traces the probable development from a 'natural' language of gesture, to a more streamlined and conventionalised system of signs, supplemented by models, dummies, and pictograms. The great (but not unimaginable) leap occurs when in the course of time it is realised that if conventional, more or less arbitrary, signs can serve to convey information and to issue commands, conventional *sounds*, with their far greater scope for variation, can serve the same purpose. After this leap has been accomplished, the later development of writing, and of the conventions of syntax and accidence, are fairly easily accounted for: and so are some of the perverted uses of language, arising in some cases from the desire to dominate or mislead, but more often from simple misconceptions of the relationships between things, ideas, and words.

Clarification of these relationships forms a major part of Englefield's second book. Believing, as he did, that faulty psychology commonly lies at the root of bad philosophy, he set out to explain the importance, at all levels of animal evolution, of *trial-and-error behaviour* for which he coined the word *peirasis*. In its simplest form (*external peirasis*) this consists in playing around with the environment until satisfaction of the animal's needs is achieved. The important step in the evolution of the thinking process comes when the animal is able to construct an internal, or mental, model of the external world on which he can carry out an analogous series of experiments. This procedure (*internal peirasis*) was clearly demonstrated in chimpanzees by the work of Köhler in 1917. Englefield's book goes on to explore the subsequent development of human inventions, which include not only tools and techniques, but language, mathematics, and scientific method. In a final section the book explores some of the less respectable activities of the human mind, such as magic and metaphysics.

Many writers, both ancient and modern, have commented on perverted uses of language in such areas as forensic pleading, sales promotion, and political propaganda. In the present book, Englefield has relatively little to say about these. Rather, he turns his attention to the abuses of language in the fields of literary criticism, religious apologetics, and philosophical discourse, which in the past have probably received less than their due share of critical scrutiny. In the first part of this volume he examines some of the more or less subtle ways in which writers on literature have used their craft, not to illuminate the writings of their predecessors, but to impress readers with their own learning, taste, and perspicacity.

The second part deals with some of the techniques which can be used to reassure worried doubters, who wish to be regarded as Christians although they can no longer accept traditional Christian beliefs. From the age of about twenty, Englefield's own attitude to religion in general and to Christianity in particular was unswervingly hostile. He had been brought up as a practising Christian, but after passing through a phase of juvenile piety, he encountered Tolstoy's heretical brand of Christianity, which influenced him for a year or so. His release came from reading the works of Guyau[1] and J. M. Robertson. Apart from his writings on Christian beliefs and Christian behaviour, Robertson remained one of Englefield's intellectual heroes, principally on account of the historical analysis in his book *The Evolution of States* (London: Watts, 1912), but also because of his practical commonsense treatment of the thinking process, set out in *Letters on Reasoning* (2nd edition, London: Watts, 1905), and abundantly illustrated in his other writings.[2]

The third part of this present book attempts to trace the parentage of various types of obscurity met with in philosophical writing, and to assess the relative importance in such writings of the difficulties of the subject itself, the desire to impress the reader, confused thinking, and misconceptions about the nature of abstraction and about the proper use of abstract nouns. Englefield's views on the function of philosophy are well displayed in a letter which he wrote to one of us in 1940:

> Knowledge is all of a piece, and thought is either clear or confused. I cannot accept the view according to which there is more than one rational way of studying the world and science is only one way. The contemporary metaphysicians who camouflage their misty speculations in quasi-scientific jargon are for me just as futile as the metaphysicians of the 19th century and later. Indeed I prefer the philosophers of the 17th and 18th centuries, the honest pre-Kantians who, for all their flounderings, did at least achieve some useful scientific results, like Descartes, Leibniz, Hume, Locke. Early ideas are necessarily crude. But it is the lucidity and honesty of these writers which make it easy now to detect their fallacies. Whereas if Kant and his followers have not been finally discredited it is largely because neither their admirers nor their critics have ever been able to understand what they were trying to say.

Before the time of Kant, the term 'Philosophy' covered Natural Philosophy—that is, what is now called Science. The immense growth of natural knowledge, and the accompanying decline in primitive systems of belief in nineteenth-century Europe, led to a separation between philosophy and science. What is now called Philosophy, and what is professed and taught in universities under that heading, is a residue, consisting largely of logic, metaphysics, and linguistic analysis. When Englefield spoke contemptuously (as he often did) of philosophy and philosophers, it was this residue that he had in mind; and it was in this context that he deplored the influence of Kant, Hegel, and their successors.

Englefield's choice of victims in all three parts of this book is determined by their usefulness as illustrative examples of literary malpractice. If they were the currently fashionable writers, it would if anything detract from his main preoccupation, which is the nature and origin of humbug. In this field, there are changes in fashion and style: but the underlying motives and stratagems change little from decade to decade. Some readers, having observed the relish with which he pours his scorn on so many well-established reputations, may ask: who, then, are authors who earned his whole-hearted respect? We have already mentioned J. M. Robertson in this connection, and have quoted Englefield's approving reference to pre-Kantian philosophers of the Enlightenment—he thought highly of Condillac, Diderot, and Voltaire, as well as of those already named. Of nineteenth-century philosophers and historians he admired in particular John Stuart Mill and H. T. Buckle's pioneer *Introduction to the History of Civilization in England*. He had great respect for Wolfgang Köhler's *Mentality of Apes*, as a model study of animal behaviour. As neurophysiologists he was beholden to Ivan Pavlov and Charles Sherrington; and as psychologists to Eugenio Rignano and Ernst Mach.

We are grateful to the late Mrs. Bärbel Selvarajan for her careful typing of the manuscript.

G. A. WELLS
D. R. OPPENHEIMER

This is a secret not known to all readers, and want of this knowledge hath occasioned much puzzling: for where a book, a chapter or paragraph hath seemed to the reader to contain Nothing, his modesty hath sometimes persuaded him that the true meaning of the author hath escaped him, instead of concluding, as in reality the fact was, that the author in the said book, etc., did truly and bona fide mean Nothing.

FIELDING

PART ONE

VERBIAGE AND LITERATURE

1

THE HAZARDS
OF FINE WRITING

If the exclusive object of speech were the expression of logical propositions, the only important qualities distinguishing one man's speech from another's would be clarity and brevity. But language is commonly used for quite other purposes. In his *Dictionary of Modern English Usage*, H. W. Fowler has an article on what he calls 'formal words'. These, he says, are not the plain English for what is meant, but language that is held more suitable for public exhibition. I remember years ago reading the autobiography of a retired judge who complained of the prevalence of formal words in this sense in the court room. When policemen give evidence, he said, they never say that they saw something as they were going down the street. Policemen speaking in court never 'go'. They always 'proceed'. And when they talked—as they often did—of watching suspects through holes in walls or fences, they always called these holes 'apertures'. The pleasure of using formal words often leads to excess, and much literary jargon originated in this way. If an idea is new and clear, it does not need to be disguised. But if it is trite or muddled, it may escape recognition by a little make-up. In such cases, the author is not merely strutting; he is making use of camouflage. In text-books, for instance, a lot of well-established and familiar ideas have to be stated, but their authors sometimes contrive to disguise the triteness. This, for instance, is how John Dewey, in his textbook on *Logic* presents the familiar idea that, by taking thought, a man may avoid the consequences of a hasty act:

> Organic biological activities end in overt actions, whose consequences are irretrievable. When an activity and its consequences can be rehearsed by representation in symbolic terms, there is no such final commitment. If the representation of the final consequence is of unwelcome quality, overt activity may be foregone, or the way of acting be replanned in such a way as to avoid the undesired outcome.[1]

Here is another example, this time from a textbook on psychology. The author says, about play:

> The significant condition for play seems to be a metabolic state which is conducive to a high level of activity when there are no stimuli with which to contend leading to the serious business of living.[2]

In other words, animals tend to play when they feel lively and have nothing better to do.

But it is writers on literature who most commonly adopt this solemn-faced tone. My next example is from a book on the Philosophy of Literary Form:

> Today . . . we are facing problems that arise from an attempt to fit private enterprise with the requirements of the citizenry as a whole. Think of the difference in magic if you confront this situation in the strategic name of 'planned economy' or, employing a different strategy, in the name of 'regimentation' . . . . If you size up a situation in the name of regimentation you decree it a different essence than if you sized it up in the name of planned economy.[3]

To "size a thing up in the name of" something seems to mean to 'call a thing' something. And to "decree a thing a different essence" means, I suppose, to regard a thing differently. What he is really saying is that we may influence some people's ideas about things by the words we use to describe them. This is true and trite. The art of the literary expert is to say such things in words which impress the reader with the writer's depth and learning.

This tendency can be seen even in histories of literature, where one might expect a plainer style in order to accommodate the many facts. My next examples are from George Sampson's *Concise History of English Literature*. This was first published (by Cambridge University Press) in 1941, and by 1955 75,000 copies had been sold. Sampson says in his preface that the book, of just over one thousand pages, is an epitome of the 14 volumes of *The Cambridge History of English Literature*, so we might expect him not to waste words. But in fact we find him writing as follows: "The immense celebrity of this work is not now very easily intelligible, nor can the possibility that Milton may have looked into it be offered as a convincing inducement to similar curiosity" (p. 178). This will on examination be found equivalent to: 'It is hard to see what made this book popular. Milton may have read it, but that is no reason why we should.'

Let us next see what he says about the Gospels:

> Nor should it be forgotten that the Gospels of the New Testament contain in little space an almost miraculous diversity of matter and unite in presenting with overwhelming simplicity a supreme tragedy. And though book differs from book in character, in aim, and in mere chronology, there is among them all a vital unity, which the least lettered reader instinctively feels. (p. 178)

The phrase 'it should not be forgotten that' merely serves to lengthen the statement. Since Sampson is rather free with the word 'miraculous' we may perhaps regard it as the literary form of 'remarkable'. 'Overwhelming' is one of those powerful adjectives of no particular meaning which are useful for the expression of feeling. 'Supreme' and 'vital' are others. The phrase 'the least lettered reader' is presumably intended to convey that *a fortiori* the learned reader must feel the same; but of course it is just the learned reader who is most likely to feel doubts about this 'vital unity'. The plain statement, without the literary style, would be something like this:

> The Gospels are brief but their contents varied. Their common theme is a tragedy which is simply portrayed. There are discrepancies between them but they have obviously much in common.

I will give one further example from Sampson:

> It is sometimes complained that Chaucer rarely rises to the level of the highest poetry. Very few poets in the world's history ever did so rise. That Chaucer had access to those heights and remained there long enough to sustain a title to greatness can only be denied by the perverse. His power to communicate poetic grace, and charm, and that large comprehension of humanity which we may call a criticism of life is clear beyond any controversy. (p. 83)

In the second sentence the last two words are unnecessary, but are inserted for the sake of balance. There is an effective rhythm in prose which helps and pleases the reader, but the skill consists in putting the rhythm into essential words. The end is defeated if useless words are inserted for the sake of the rhythm. Note too the circumlocution. Instead of asserting simply that Chaucer had access to those heights, Sampson feels that there is some emphasis added by saying that those who deny it are perverse. The formula is this. The writer wishes to assert that coal is black. He starts off, 'That coal is black', and then has a choice of formulas—'is generally admitted', 'is scarcely to be denied', 'can be denied only by the perverse', and so on. This device enables us to vary the monotony of our trite remarks. Now look at Sampson's final sentence: put into its simple form, it would be: 'He can communicate poetic grace, and charm, and that large comprehension of humanity, etc.' In this form the proposition is more likely to make the reader query the meaning. Sampson's method here is to use a very strong form of assertion and reserve it for the end of the sentence. The kindling doubt in the reader's mind is swiftly quenched. The last impression in the mind is the emphatic and contemptuous rejection of demurrers. With the order inverted the last impression would have been the egregious proposition.

The literary writer is often concerned to persuade us to accept his authority. One method he has of doing this is to write with extravagant praise about men of established reputation. The effect of this is to raise his prestige and so make his assertions on other matters more acceptable. Homer, Plato, Dante, and Shakespeare are common subjects for this kind of writing. To question their supreme merit might suggest inability to appreciate. An attitude of superiority to certain writers of second rank may be just as effective as a devout attitude to the acknowledged great ones and many an ambitious writer has tried to score a point by a sneer at Rousseau or Voltaire or John Stuart Mill. For instance, T. S. Eliot mentions the influence of Montaigne on Pascal. Montaigne was disinclined to believe in witchcraft, but as most of his contemporaries believed in it, and he could find no conclusive argument against it, he did not profess knowledge on the matter, but merely questioned the propriety of roasting people alive on the chance. Pascal's argument *for* orthodox

Christianity is based on a like scepticism. Since we cannot be sure that the Christian doctrine of Hell is not true, we are well advised—says Pascal—to believe. Eliot does not explain the arguments of Pascal. It is wise of him not to do so, for they would be unacceptable to many of his readers. The authority of Pascal is more important than his arguments, and Eliot therefore tells us that he was one of the finest mathematical minds of any time.[4] Instead of discussing arguments, Eliot comments on the comparative size and importance of different French writers:

> Had Montaigne been an ordinary life-sized sceptic, a small man like Anatole France, or even a greater man like Renan, or even like the greatest sceptic of all, Voltaire, this 'influence' [i.e. of Montaigne] would be to the discredit of Pascal; but if Montaigne had been no more than Voltaire, he could not have affected Pascal at all. (p. 410)

No reasons are given for this estimate of comparative size and for the discredit which falls upon those who are influenced by Voltaire. But we can understand Eliot's feelings without his giving any reasons.

Another common method consists in attaching disagreeable images, or words with disagreeable emotional associations, to ideas, attitudes, or policies one wants to discredit. We are all familiar with writings which tell us that materialism, for instance, is dreary, cold, and ghost-like. Eliot writes in this manner of the sceptics:

> The majority of mankind is lazy-minded, incurious, absorbed in vanities, and tepid in emotion, and is therefore incapable of either much doubt or much faith; and when the ordinary man calls himself a sceptic or an unbeliever, that is ordinarily a simple pose, cloaking a disinclination to think anything out to a conclusion. (pp. 411-12)

There is perhaps a certain amount of lazy-mindedness and uncuriosity among the faithful. When the 'ordinary man' calls himself a believer, that may mean all sorts of different things, but it does not perhaps very often mean that he has a particularly strong bent for thinking things out to a conclusion. But, of course, the expression is a little vague. Thinking things out to a conclusion need not signify a very great intellectual effort, as all depends on the point at which the conclusion is reached and the quality of the 'thinking out'. I shall deal more fully below with the kind of emotional colouring on which Eliot here relies.

Let me give one final example from Eliot. It illustrates almost perfectly the kind of fatuous statement that passes for literary criticism: "Blake did not have that more Mediterranean gift of form which knows how to borrow, as Dante borrowed his theory of the soul" (pp. 320–321). Dante, then, because he lived near the Mediterranean, knew how to borrow his theory of the soul. Most people, whether they live near the Mediterranean or the Arctic Ocean, are reduced to borrowing their theory of the soul, whether they have the gift which knows how to do it or not.

The evils of style I have been indicting have long been recognised. Schopenhauer, one of the most lucid writers Germany has ever produced, wrote of them as follows in his little essay on 'Writing and Style'.

> German authors would, all of them, profit from realising that, although one should, wherever possible, think like a great mind, one should on the other hand speak the same language as everyone else. What is needed are ordinary words to say unusual things. But in fact authors do the opposite. We find them concerned to conceal trivial ideas with elegant words and to deck their very ordinary thoughts in the most unusual expressions.[5]

The abuse may have been particularly widespread in the Hegelian Germany of Schopenhauer's day. (He once said that if you can read Hegel without feeling that you are in the mad-house, then you ought to be in the mad-house[6]). But to my mind things have not changed for the better, either in Germany or elsewhere.

Let us next consider the use of words to stimulate emotion. The following two statements express the same idea:

1. The train arrived at St. Pancras at 11:55 p.m.

2. Shortly before midnight the mammoth engine came snorting under the lofty vaults of the familiar terminus.

The first is plain and fairly precise, the second coloured and imprecise. The comparison of an engine to a mammoth, though uninformative, is not, however, purposeless. The extinct mammal has, for various reasons, come to be associated with impressive bigness. We may read of a 'mammoth ship', a 'mammoth building', a 'mammoth enterprise', though in fact a ship or a building no bigger than a mammoth would be rather small, and the size of an undertaking does not admit of comparison with that of an animal. There is, however, an emotional reaction to things larger than ourselves, and by long custom certain words have acquired the power of stirring this emotion. I propose to illustrate the use of words for emotional effect with some passages from Ruskin's *The Crown of Wild Olive* (1866). The first is from the Preface:

> Just in the very rush and murmur of the first spreading currents, the human wretches of the place cast their street and house foulness; heaps of dust and slime, and broken shreds of old metal, and rags of putrid clothes; they having neither energy to cart it away, nor decency enough to dig it into the ground, thus shed into the stream, to diffuse what venom of it will float and melt, far away, in all places where God meant those waters to bring joy and health.

Ruskin's intention is to arouse in the minds of his reader the feeling of aversion which he experienced himself. Refuse of dust, slime, pieces of metal and clothing had been deposited in a stream. The plain statement does not necessarily produce the desired effect, so the expression 'putrid clothes' is added to suggest that these objects pollute the water. But clothes, whether of wool or cotton, do not putrefy, though like all organic substances, including the trees and grass, they decay in time. And the polluting effect of dust and slime depends on what they consist of. The final reference to God's intention also betrays that the description as given does not produce its effect by the plain meaning of the terms used. But the words 'slime', 'rags', 'putrid', 'foulness', 'venom', have all more or less strong emotional colouring, for which purpose rather than for any nicety of signification they are here chosen.

The description of the present state of Carshalton is in contrast with the preceding passage describing its earlier condition:

> No clearer or diviner waters ever sang with constant lips of the hand which 'giveth rain from heaven'; no pastures ever lightened in spring time with more passionate blossoming; no sweeter homes ever hallowed the heart of the passer-by with their pride of peaceful gladness—fain-hidden—yet full-confessed.

The alliteration of the final phrases and the use of such words as 'divine', 'passionate', and 'sweet', in relation to waters, blossoming and homes, have but one possible purpose, the stirring of emotion, for here the terms have no intellectual content at all. 'Divine waters' simply means that Ruskin liked them. 'Passionate blossoming' indicates more vaguely that Ruskinian emotional reaction to the flowering fields. 'Sweet homes' suggests that he regarded the buildings in question with a certain complacency. Further on, however, he refers to the inhabitants of these 'sweet homes' as 'human herds'. The word 'herd' applied to men has a peculiar emotional colouring, here required to indicate Ruskin's change of attitude.

He continues:

> The place remains . . . . nearly unchanged in its larger features; but, with deliberate mind I say, that I have never seen anything so ghastly in its inner tragic meaning—not in Pisan Maremma,—not by Campagna tomb,—not by the sand-isles of the Torcellan shore,—as the slow stealing of aspects of reckless, indolent, animal neglect, over the delicate sweetness of that English scene: nor is any blasphemy or impiety—any frantic saying or godless thought—more appalling to me, using the best power of judgment I have to discern its sense and scope, than the insolent defiling of those springs by the human herds that drink of them.

In addition to the simple emotional expression which appears in the use of words like 'ghastly', 'tragic', 'frantic', 'godless', 'appalling', 'impiety', 'blasphemy', there is here to be noted another element of style. The Italian references are apparently quite irrelevant, but by no means superfluous, for they are intended to enhance the prestige of the writer. Our propositions are more readily accepted by those who respect our judgment. If we can, by choice of terms or illustrations, convey to our hearers that we are profound thinkers or peculiarly well-equipped experts, they will very likely be willing to accept on our unsupported authority propositions the truth of which is not otherwise evident to them. Ruskin is emphasising his wide experience and his expert acquaintance with the obscurer phases of mediaeval art. The more he can impress his reader that he is a man of vast authority, the greater will be the weight attaching to his anathema.

The orator often relies not merely on an authoritarian air,

but also on deception. The art of persuasion may, of course, theoretically be practised in favour of true as well as of false propositions. But, because the coherence of true propositions is in itself persuasive, the art is more frequently employed in favour of false ones. The falsity of a proposition can ultimately be shown only by its inconsistency with propositions known on other grounds to be true. True propositions are always consistent with one another. Hence to persuade people into believing a true proposition, the principal thing is to make it perfectly clear, so that its consistency with the body of accepted knowledge is exhibited. But if it is desired to gain acceptance for a false proposition, its inconsistency with the body of accepted knowledge must be concealed. Hence the clear statement of false propositions is seldom likely to persuade. Certain of them are more readily acceptable because they flatter us, and these are very convenient to the rhetorician, who chooses them to show their consistency with what he is defending. Ruskin's lecture on war (included in *The Crown of Wild Olive*) was addressed to young cadets and provides a good example of this flattering method. To quote it would be a lengthy business, but I can summarise it, as follows:

1. War is conducive to good art.

2. Art is a symptom of national excellence.

3. Hence war is conducive to national excellence.

4. You soldiers are mighty fine fellows.

5. I, as an artist, am a symptom of national excellence, if not part of the national excellence itself.

The argument is as follows: all these propositions are consistent, so, if you accept one, you will readily accept the others. But I can prove the first by showing its consistency with certain less general propositions:

a. Greece and Egypt were warlike nations and produced great art.

b. Rome was not [!] a warlike nation and produced none.

c. The only warlike nations today are England and France, and they alone are producing any good art.

The acceptance of these three propositions might prove difficult for an audience of historians, but could not reasonably be supposed to present serious difficulties to Ruskin's audience of Woolwich cadets. Thus by skilful arrangement does he cajole his youthful warriors into respect for his own particular hobby. The method consists in showing that the proposition to be proved is consistent with propositions which (true or not) flatter the hearer or are outside the range of his knowledge and in themselves indifferent to him.

Another example from the same collection of essays illustrates a different method. It is from the beginning of the lecture entitled 'Traffic':

> My good Yorkshire friends, you asked me down here among your hills that I might talk to you about this Exchange you are going to build: but earnestly and seriously asking you to pardon me, I am going to do nothing of the kind. I cannot talk, or at least can say very little, about this same Exchange. I must talk of quite other things, though not willingly;—I could not deserve your pardon, if, when you invited me to speak on one subject, I wilfully spoke on another. But I cannot speak, to purpose, of anything about which I do not care; and most simply and sorrowfully I have to tell you, in the outset, that I do *not* care about this Exchange of yours.

There is a noticeable difference between Ruskin's manner of address to an audience of 'high-born' military cadets and one of low-born Bradford merchants. It is surprising that the gifted lecturer, having found the defence of war so simple, should find that of an Exchange so difficult. Having seen with what facility he marshalled the proofs in the former case, we cannot readily believe that he could not have done as well in this if he had chosen. But there is persuasion by bullying as well as by cajolery. In either case it is necessary to arouse respect in the mind of the hearer.

> Believe me, without farther instance, I could show you, in all time, that every nation's vice, or virtue, was written in its art: the soldiership of early Greece; the sensuality of late Italy; the visionary religion of Tuscany; the splendid human energy and beauty of Venice. I have no time to do this tonight . . . . I will simply assure you that whatever is good or great in Egypt, and Syria, and India, is just as good or

great for the same reasons as the buildings on our side of the
Bosphorus.

In a gathering of Egyptologists and Orientalists such a statement might have required elucidation, but before the merchants of Bradford it was safe. It was only necessary that the
authority of the speaker should be well and firmly established. This was how it was done:

> It was the selling of absolution that ended the Mediaeval faith; and I
> can tell you more, it is the selling of absolution which, to the end of
> time, will mark false Christianity.

It is now the voice of the prophet speaking: 'Verily, verily, I
say unto you . . .' The number of Roman Catholics in the audience was probably very small, so that the proposition that
the mediaeval faith was ended would safely pass without
challenge.

> We English have beautiful little quiet ways of buying absolution,
> whether in low Church or high, far more cunning than any of Tetzel's
> trading.

The Bradfordians, not being likely to have heard of Tetzel,
were expected to be impressed.

But let me return to methods which involve flattering the
reader. As already noted, literary art may be used not only to
serve error, but also to defend what is true or discredit what is
false. To satirise an erroneous idea, for instance, it is only
necessary to put it very clearly and draw the inevitable conclusions from it, assuming the tone of conviction of one pro-
pounding with confidence. The following extract from the article 'Abraham' in Voltaire's *Dictionnaire philosophique* will
illustrate:

> It is hardly 400 years since the Flood and the time has arrived in which
> we place Abraham's journey among the Egyptians. This people will
> have been extremely ingenious and hard-working to have invented the
> arts and all the sciences in so short a time, to have tamed the Nile and
> changed the whole face of the country . . . .

It is here unnecessary to exaggerate. It is sufficient merely to
state the consequences clearly. The ironical manner consists
in assuming a serious tone and pretending to believe in the

evidently ridiculous conclusion. This flatters the reader by leaving with him the task of criticism.

I have illustrated the tendency to use pretentious words instead of more common ones, and some of the other methods which writers use to persuade us to accept their authority—such as suggesting deep learning, appealing to prejudice (making theories to fit what people want to believe), or simply adopting the authoritarian air of 'admire ye groundlings!' The passage from Voltaire illustrates that such methods are less needed for the defence of the truth, and so we shall do well to regard their occurrence with some suspicion.

Language serves many purposes: it expresses the emotions, it is used to terrify and intimidate, to excite and to bemuse; and also to give a sober description of facts. This last function would be much better served if the instrument were less well adapted to the others.

2

VICES OF LITERARY CRITICISM

From Antiquity to the European Renaissance, poets (some poets, at all events) were held in very high esteem. At the lowest, they were entertainers in times when public entertainment had to be sought for. At the highest, they thrilled their audiences with stories of the gods or of bygone heroes, using rhythmic utterance and antique diction to stir men's emotions. In ancient Greece, Homer was revered as an almost divine personage. In Rome, the same word served for soothsayer and poet, and in the Middle Ages the writings of Virgil had magical attributes.

By the nineteenth century, things had changed. There were other sources of entertainment. The poet's role as a teacher had largely been usurped by writers of cold, uninspiring prose, and 'men of letters' were becoming aware that the sort of questions with which they had long been accustomed to deal were now beginning to be tackled by scientists. Seeing their authority challenged in what they regarded as their special domain, the men of letters reacted by claiming that they possessed a kind of superior insight denied to the mere scientist. Carlyle, for instance, wrote of the man of letters as "our most important modern person" who endeavours "to speak forth the inspiration" in him—"the inspired wisdom of a Heroic Soul". "Intrinsically it is the same function which the old generations named a man Prophet, Priest, Divinity, for doing."[1] Wordsworth, discussing the relation of poetry to science, declares that it is the former which is "the first and last of all knowledge".[2] Shelley contrasts poetry, as "something divine . . . , at once the centre and circumference of all knowledge", with the "grosser sciences" (i.e. physical science) and also with psychology and sociology—"that application of analytical reasoning to the aberrations of society, which it is now atempted to exalt over the direct expression of the inventive and creative faculty itself". He also calls a poem "the very image of life expressed in its eternal truth", and says:

> All the authors of revolutions in opinion are not only necessarily poets as they are inventors, nor even as their words unveil the permanent analogy of things by images which participate in the life of truth; but as their periods are harmonious and rhythmical, and contain in themselves the elements of verse; being the echo of the eternal music.[3]

The most obvious thing about this writing is the desire to glorify poetry and the poet. Shelley does so by inventing all kinds of abstract entities: the eternal music, the permanent analogy of things, life in its eternal truth, and so on.

The poet, writing about his own art, is naturally inclined to exaggerate its importance. Were he to undertake to analyse the mind and motives of the professional clown or strip-tease artist he would approach the matter in a different spirit. On the other hand the strip-tease artist could no doubt find good reasons for believing her art noble and beneficent, affording delight and edification to an unhappy generation of businessmen suffering from overwork and mental strain. And her manager would support her claims. In the same way we find that the professional literary theorist has, as a rule, as high an opinion of the status of the poet as the poet himself; and this is understandable, for the prestige of the critic must depend on the importance of the subject of his criticism. The critic is for the poet what the priest is for the deity.

The affinity of the poet to the prophet had long been recognised and, from the point of view of Carlyle, Ruskin, Emerson, Arnold, and other minor prophets of the period, it was reasonable to extend the connection to the essayist and literary or art critic. The man of letters in fact stepped into the shoes of the poet. I have argued elsewhere[4] that some of the most striking features of poetic form—rhythm and alliteration, for instance—were devices of primitive composers to make easier the task of memorising compositions deemed of special importance; and that when writing made the effort of memorising unnecessary, the old form continued to be used with more solemn and sacred compositions in accordance with the principle of the special sanctity of the archaic. The invention of printing and the wide circulation of printed books finally made it altogether unnecessary to commit the compositions of the wise to memory. The man of letters is distinguished from the poet merely in that he writes in prose. There is no further need for the aids of line, stanza, and metre, but the advantages of a special language are retained. It does not help the memory, but it impresses the reader. Rhythmical and alliterative prose, especially if the language has a touch of the archaic, produces an emotional response inherited from a remote ancestry accustomed to associate such elements with solemnity and devotion.

Now oracular utterances are commonly ambiguous or obscure. But the fact that we are unable to understand does not normally detract from their emotional effect. On the contrary, this obscurity is another characteristic of the pronouncements of seers and prophets. It may even enhance their prestige, and the seers and prophets are tempted to exploit this effect. Not only are they able in this way to impress their hearers at very little expense, but the ambiguity of their prophecies disguises their non-fulfilment. And where they professed to reveal the words of God it encouraged belief, for it was to be expected that the language of God would differ from the vulgar speech of ordinary mortals.

The poet is also a seer, or was long so regarded, and the belief that his utterances need to be interpreted is a natural result of such a view. In later times, the commentator or critic sees his task as that of supplying the interpretation. The poet, like the prophet, speaks to the vulgar in parables, "that seeing they may not see, and hearing they may not understand". But unto the critics and commentators it is given "to know the mysteries" (Luke 8:9–10). Thus have the men of letters supposed that their function is almost as august as that of the poets, and their status superior to that of the scientist.

We must recognise that there is an academic rivalry at the universities, where a distinction is drawn between science and 'the Arts'. The two disciplines are regarded as alternative types of education and culture, and so the question arises which of the two is more valuable. The value of science is obvious to all, whereas the value of the 'fine arts' and more especially 'literature', except as a leisure occupation, is less obvious. It is true that literary degrees are recognised as qualifications for many desirable jobs, especially teaching jobs. But why should we need teachers of literature unless literature had some value, and were worth teaching? The answer of those responsible at the universities for organising such teaching is that their subject is something of much greater importance than a mere form of entertainment. If it were not for this need to vindicate the social or ethical value of literature there would be less of the endless discussion about the nature of poetry. We do not often hear similar discussions about the nature of dancing. The dancer or choreographer is content to receive the applause of those whom he delights without pretending to contribute anything to their intellectual or moral stature. He does not claim to reveal the mysteries of the universe or to elevate the religious or philosophical consciousness of the listener. But the poet is still in many cases inclined to regard himself as the heir of the long line of seers and prophets. He has a message. Not an intelligible message about mere matters of fact, but a revelation of something higher, deeper, more immense, more exalted, more profound.

I. A. Richards in his book *Principles of Literary Criticism* speaks of the arts in general, but is more particularly concerned with literature, and insists that this business of literature and literary criticism is of first-rate importance. He says:

> The arts are our storehouse of recorded values. They spring from and perpetuate hours in the lives of exceptional people, when their control and command of experience is at its highest, hours when the varying possibilities of existence are most clearly seen and the different activities which may arise are most exquisitely reconciled . . . Very simple experiences—a cold bath in an enamelled tin, or running for a train—may to some extent be compared without elaborate vehicles; . . . But subtle or recondite experiences are for most men incommunicable and indescribable . . . In the arts we find the record in the only form in which these things can be recorded of the experiences

which have seemed worth having to the most sensitive and
discriminating persons. Through the obscure perception of this fact
the poet has been regarded as a seer and the artist as a priest . . . The
arts, if rightly approached, supply the best data available for deciding
what experiences are more valuable than others.[5]

The attentive reader will notice that the whole argument
depends on the meaning of the adjectives, which is very far
from clear. "Exceptional people": he cannot mean to use the
word 'exceptional' in its usual sense, for it would then include
criminals and lunatics. We must assume that he means 'excellent people', while omitting to say how we are to recognise
them. This is important, for many might think that the most
successful artists and poets have not always been the most ad-
mirable, the most virtuous, or even the most intelligent of
people. "Command of experience at its highest": here again
there is a suggestion of supreme excellence; yet, unless we
know in what the 'excellence' consists, the superlative
'highest' conveys no more than 'deepest', 'longest' or 'fat-
test'. "Different activities exquisitely reconciled": once
more, the adverb seems to imply some kind of excellence, but
what does it in fact mean? How can a reconciliation be ex-
quisite? "Experiences which have seemed worth having to the
most sensitive and discriminating persons": 'sensitive' is ambiguous. And in the usual sense of the word we should not
specially value the experiences of the most sensitive persons.
Such people are sometimes rather tiresome. But in the literary
jargon the word is more vague. It is usually a laudatory term,
and that is evidently the intention here. But how the degree of
this kind of sensitivity can be measured we are not told.
'Discriminating' must here be supposed to mean 'able to
distinguish the "excellent" from the "bad" '. But who will
tell us which are the truly discriminating people? Again,
"The arts . . . supply the best data available for deciding what
experiences are more valuable than others". And that is the
final word. The arts represent the best records of the best experiences of the best men. The rest of us may manage to say
something intelligible about a cold bath or running for a
train, but the subtle and recondite experiences of the exceptional people who control experience at its highest and ex-

quisitely reconcile their different activities—these are accessible only to the master-critic. "The arts, if rightly approached . . ." There is indeed the difficulty, and is where we need the guidance of the professional critic. Critics are extremely important people. If nothing else has been made clear, this at least the simplest reader cannot miss.

The all too obvious purpose of this kind of writing is to win the approval of the reader, to establish a reputation for fine writing, for profound understanding, for critical acumen, and so on. The great danger faced by the superior poet and the discerning critic is lack of popularity. They do not, of course, seek the applause of the vulgar, but they must have an audience, and the gradual diminution of the highbrow public is a serious matter. Richards says:

> The gulf between what is preferred by the majority and what is accepted as excellent by the most qualified opinion . . . appears likely to become threatening in the near future. (*Ibid*., p. 36)

Who or what is threatened? Clearly the authority and prestige of what regards itself as 'qualified opinion'. Richards fears what he calls "a collapse of values, a transvaluation by which popular taste replaces trained discrimination". What then is 'trained discrimination', and by whom is it trained? Here there is implied an analogy with science and technology where there exists a body of established principles and methods, which has been tested again and again in all parts of the world by thousands of practitioners working in circumstances where failure would announce itself unambiguously. These principles have been recorded and can be imparted to students by those who have studied and learned them. Of course, on the frontiers of every established science there is uncertainty, theorising and exploration, but in physics, chemistry, and biology there is a wide field of well-established principles and methods. No such field exists in the domain with which Richards is concerned. If we understood better the principles of human behaviour—let us call it 'psychology'—then we might expect to have experts who could explain the effects of certain works of art or literature on this or that type of person. At present there are no such experts.

In another work, while discussing sentimentalism in poetry, Richards refers to "an inappropriate response".[6] Now we can understand what is meant by this expression when we are talking of normal animal behaviour. It implies that we understand the situation, that we know what are the needs of the animal, and that we can see that the behaviour adopted is not likely to bring about the satisfaction of those needs. When we read the accounts of Köhler's chimpanzees it is usually easy to distinguish between the appropriate and the inappropriate responses, but when the behaviour of men is in question it is not as a rule so easy. We cannot always say what the need is which prompts the behaviour, and so cannot tell whether it is satisfied or not. In particular, where such obscure needs are involved as those which prompt the reading or writing of poetry, what ground can we have for saying whether the 'response' is appropriate, especially as it is very hard, as a rule, to find out what the response is, as it is often largely unexpressed. And how are we to know whether the emotional reaction of a reader to a poem is appropriate? Even if we have reliable means of knowing what the emotional reaction is, we only compare it with our own or somebody else's. Who determines the standard? Richards seems to suppose that he knows precisely what kind of emotional response should be 'called forth' by any and every poem, and that he can accordingly judge at once whether any particular reader's reaction is the correct one.

Appropriate responses to poetry are, according to Richards, a matter of the highest importance:

> The basis of morality, as Shelley insisted, is laid not by preachers but by poets. Bad taste and crude responses are not mere flaws in an otherwise admirable person. They are actually a root evil from which other defects follow. No life can be excellent in which the elementary responses are disorganised and confused.[7]

Bad taste means liking the wrong pictures or reading the wrong books. 'Crude responses' might mean many different things. What exactly is the difference between a root evil and an evil which follows from it? Has this literary critic analysed human nature so as to be able to determine the roots of evil and good, and the consequences which follow from them? If so, he should begin by telling us all about it. If he has not, then these vague generalisations mean nothing at all.

These passages from Richards are typical of a good deal of twentieth-century literary criticism, which can be seen, on examination, to possess the following characteristics. It is a kind of discourse, but it lacks all intelligible sequence and is often made up of quite meaningless sentences. But the words employed are often familiar, and include many taken from scientific writings. Authorities are frequently cited, though the relevance of the citation is generally obscure, and the passages cited are often equally obscure. Lucid passages occur at intervals, expressing the emotions of the writer. Current fashions in philosophy, psychology and literary theory are alluded to, not in order to explain or criticise them, but rather to convey a notion of the author's awareness of all the latest ideas. References are often so vague that they convey nothing of interest, but do not expose the author to the danger of contradiction.

Wimsatt and Brooks's *Literary Criticism: A Short History* (New York and London: Knopf, 1957) illustrates all these tendencies both in the passages quoted, and in those which represent the opinions of the two authors. They say, for instance, that

> The symbolist movement may be described as the effort to bring poetry to the condition of music—indeed Valéry did so describe it in 1926. Mallarmé's poetry is clearly musical in this sense, words being organized and orchestrated almost as if they were musical notes. (p. 593)

"In this sense": convenient phrase! But they have not given a hint of what sense. They say that words are "organized" and "orchestrated" like musical notes. These two words can in this context mean nothing. If 'organised' means 'arranged'—and it is hard to see what you can do with words except arrange them in some chosen order—then the statement is absurd, for words are not arranged like notes. To say that the words are orchestrated is even more absurd. In choral settings different voices may be singing different words at the same time and this does have some analogy with orchestration. But this is not the work of the poet, but of the composer who sets the words to music. It will hardly be suggested that the works of the 'symbolist' poets are more easily adapted for this purpose than, say, the Psalms.

In fact, of course, music is quite different from poetry; the only thing they have in common is rhythmic sound. It is this which can link verse and melody. There is, it is true, tonal variation in speech, but it varies with the speaker and the dialect, and in poetry it is determined by the reader and not the poet. The poet has no means of indicating to the reader how the voice should rise and fall, or the force with which each word should be uttered. When a poem is set to music the tonal variation is imposed on the words by the melody and is usually quite different from that which would be natural in ordinary speech. If Valéry and Mallarmé really did try to bring poetry closer to music it can only have been by suppressing the meaning. Music can express emotion, but it cannot express ideas unless by the direct imitation of familiar sounds. Poetry expresses emotion almost entirely by the use of words which convey ideas. The reciter of poetry can, of course, express emotion by the tone of his voice and the expression on his face, but neither of these constitutes any part of the poet's composition.

It is often supposed that certain combinations of sounds, of vowels and consonants, can convey something even in the entire absence of any conventional meaning, and this must have formed the basis of the 'symbolist' theory. But this can be tested. One has only to listen to a poem recited in a foreign language. If the reader avoids supplying the emotional expression and reads in a level monotone, while pronouncing every word very clearly, then no listener who is quite ignorant of the language will be able to guess what the poet was trying to express. If this is true—and anybody can make the experiment—poetry consisting of word-sequences without meaning can owe any effect it produces solely to the expression of the reader.

Wimsatt and Brooks say further that, for Mallarmé, words were "much more than signs" and that "used evocatively and ritualistically they are the means by which we are inducted into an ideal world". This "ideal world" seems to be a latter-day substitute for Heaven, and the religious flavour of the words 'induct' and 'ritual' makes them appropriate here. That something of the kind was what Mallarmé had in mind appears from the following quotation which they give from the poet:

> Poetry is . . . the expression, by means of human language restored to its essential rhythm, of the mysterious sense of the aspects of existence: it endows our sojourn with authenticity and constitutes the sole spiritual task. (p. 593)

Though they do not suggest that this is just pure verbiage, they do express a certain uneasiness. They say:

> Thus symbolist poetry at its apogee threatens to purify itself out of existence. If the pressure for pure meaning is pressed unremittingly, the poem is finally detached from reality and becomes knowledge of *nothing*! (p. 596)

Why "at its apogee"? They merely mean 'in the end' or 'ultimately' not that at its perigee it is out of danger! How does one press the pressure for meaning? Is this just slovenly writing? And when they say that the poem becomes detached from reality, is this the literary jargon for 'the poem is meaningless'? And may we perhaps translate "knowledge of nothing" by 'undiluted piffle'?

Later, after quoting some lines of Yeats about rags and bones and the slut who keeps the till, the same authors say that these lines

> point to an important fact about Yeats's poetry: there is a real working dualism—real oppositions as distinguished from merely opposed positions in an abstract dialectic. The poetry can aspire to the reduction of all things to 'intellectual fire' for the very good reason that the materials to be consumed are not wraiths of uninflammable moonshine. (Like the French symbolists before him, Yeats had learned, in part from Nietzsche, the uses of tension and conflict in art.) The materials that make up the poems have enough substance to resist, and when ignited, to feed, combustion. (p. 606)

Was it necessary to learn from Nietzsche the uses of conflict in art? Is not conflict one of the commonest forms of human activity, and have not all artists and poets in all times made use of it? What is an "abstract dialectic"? Is this yet another term for verbiage? "Wraiths of uninflammable moonshine" must be another. What is the substance in a poem which resists combustion? And what is the nature of the combustion which it resists? Is it possible to make any kind of sense out of all this? I hardly think it is expected of the reader. He is expected to admire but not to understand.

I turn now to another well-known critic, F. R. Leavis. He prefaces his *New Bearings in English Poetry* with a quotation to the effect that "what we cannot understand, it is a very common, and indeed a very natural thing, for us to undervalue". This is no doubt true. But it is also true that what we do not understand but find extolled by apparently important people, we will make a show of admiring in order not to display our own incapacity or want of taste. It is further true that what is meaningless cannot be understood by anybody. It would, on the whole, be better if we all confessed frankly our inability to understand whenever that was in fact the case. But it is too often assumed—and critics are apt to encourage the assumption—that profound thoughts can be expressed only in obscure language which the superior minds alone can expect to understand. Hence the danger to the unwary student of claiming to have penetrated the meaning of what is in truth devoid of any.

Leavis's book contains many pieces typical of modern literary criticism. His appraisal, for instance, of Eliot's poem *Portrait of a Lady* evidently aims at giving the impression of enthusiastic approval, but the actual terms which he uses are too vague to convey anything that could be confirmed or denied by a study of the poem. In quoting his words I will italicise those of dubious meaning:

> In *Portrait of a Lady* the *poise* is more *subtle*, and it is maintained with sure and *exquisite delicacy*. The poet's *command* both of his *experience* and of his *technique* (if we can distinguish) is *perfect*.

He then quotes nine lines from the poem and continues:

> The *flexibility* and *control* of this are maintained throughout the poem. The utterances of the lady are in the idiom and *cadence* of modern speech, and they go perfectly with the *movement* of the verse, which, for all its freedom and variety, is nevertheless very *strict* and *precise*. The poet is as close to the contemporary world as any novelist could be, and his formal verse medium makes possible a concentration and a directness, audacities of transition and *psychological notation*, such as are forbidden to the novelist.[8]

The italicised words would all be clear enough in an intelligible context, but here they can only be used in a metaphorical or technical sense at which we can only guess. Would it be possible to take any ten lines from another poet, any one from Chaucer to Browning, and say whether they exhibit 'flexibility', 'control', 'movement', 'strictness' or 'precision'? These are all useful words in an appropriate context, but what can they mean when applied to verse? Poets do, of course, have their peculiar styles, just like composers, so that with practice we can make a good guess at the author or composer of a work not previously known to us. But when this is really so, it is possible to point out the recognisable features, certain rhythms, words, phrases, grammatical peculiarities, rhymes, alliteration, archaisms. These things can be recognised, counted, described without ambiguity. But who can say where there is 'flexibility' or 'control'? There are, it is true, qualities in poetry of which we are aware although they are difficult to describe. To say that a melody is beautiful is not a meaningless statement. If sincere it describes an effect in the listener which may be due more to the nature or state of mind of the listener than to the objective character of the music. If there are discoverable objective features in music or poetry which contribute to produce this sense of 'beauty', then technical terms to denote them are necessary. But a technical term is useless unless we have some practical way of determining its meaning. In science technical terms are indispensable, but the meaning of such terms can be explained only by reference to the thing named. Or if a definition is employed, then the terms of the definition must be explained by practical demonstration. The literary jargon relies on the use of words which are sufficiently familiar but have such a vague and variable reference that in the context, which is equally vague, they remain strictly meaningless. If we are to have technical terms for the description of poetry they must be defined by reference to actual examples. What, for example, is 'cadence'? What is 'psychological notation'? Let us have examples, lines of verse from different poets, in different languages, and let the cadence or notation be altered without altering the meaning or the phraseology. If the study of poetry is in fact worth while, then we should study it seriously.

In this type of writing the words make up sentences which are grammatically acceptable, contain subject and predicate, and have the outward aspect of propositions, but they remain for the most part uninterpretable with reference to any kind of reality. The scientist is always being pulled up by the need to translate his theories into experimental data. The philosopher and the literary critic lack this material check and are in constant danger of floating off into regions of pure speculation and losing all contact with concrete experience. They cannot really think without the aid of non-verbal images, but as they recede from the region of measurable events, the bonds are loosened, the order prescribed by experience is forgotten, and the sequence of real events is dissolved and the fragments recombined into monsters and fantasms.

The exposure of the emptiness of this kind of writing is hindered by the more and more prevalent practice of make-believe. Writers are sometimes mainly concerned to give the impression that they are clever, imaginative, learned, profound, witty, important, well-known, etc., and there are so many simple readers who accept very inadequate criteria, that this impression may easily be given. Every week one may read in the newspapers or magazines articles in which, whatever the ostensible topic, the manifest aim of the writer is to create a favourable impression in the reader, to suggest knowledge by allusion, authority by manner, high connections by personal reminiscences, profound understanding by oracular and obscure language. Such articles often throw very little light on the subject supposed to be under discussion. But the reader too often reads with a similar aim. He does not look for information or enlightenment but rather seeks to feel himself cultured, knowledgeable, intelligent, and supposes that he must be clever to be able to read such clever articles.

Literary study and discussion need not be futile. It will be most valuable when it is naive, when each participant gives an honest account of his own feelings. It is of least value when an attempt is made to estimate the value of a writing by reference to some theoretical standard, or when such a critical standard is itself the subject of dispute. The whole question of aesthetic (as of moral) principles depends on whether we have to rely on the consensus of opinion as to what is right or wrong, good or bad, or whether there is some independent criterion. The critic, as a rule, sets himself up as an authority who judges directly the worth of a work of art, and not merely as one who counts heads. Since he cannot admit the authority of the common voice, he must depend on some other criterion, but it is extremely hard to say what this can be; for if some external features are laid down, some describable and measurable characters in the work itself, then it is found that a new criterion has to be erected in each generation. This would not be so bad if it were not for the fact that certain old works of art continue to be treated with reverence. Hence the new criterion must somehow be made to fit in not only with the latest fashion but also with the established classics. It would not be impossible, perhaps, to draw up a set of rules which would make the poetry of Mallarmé first-class, but it is difficult to find a definition of excellence that will include Homer and Shakespeare as well. This seems to be the reason why all attempts to erect general principles of literary criticism involve contradictions and obscurities.

If we wish to understand the poet and his work, then we must not take at their face value utterances by interested parties about the supreme importance of poetry. We have to recognise that there must be some motive, or some driving force, behind the activities of any man, and that the poet and the critic can be no exception. If we are not prepared to recognise that they are men with human impulses and desires, we shall certainly never arrive at anything but empty formulas signifying nothing. Poetry, drama, and all forms of literature may form subjects for sensible discussion, even for scientific study—for the distinction between science and arts is merely traditional, and any study comes within the scope of science if it is based on observation, the establishment of facts, the construction and testing of generalisations, the making of experiments and the use of rational hypotheses. One reason why books on literature are often frustrating is that they are not written in the scientific spirit. Critics do not give simple, intelligible reasons for saying why they find a book dull or interesting, but speak of its metaphysical intentionality, its authenticity, its phenomenological dimensions, its structure and function, its ambivalences, dialectic and eschatology; its momentum, its overtones and undertones, its symbolism and paradoxes, its reverberance, its resonance, relevance and transcendence. And their readers are content to borrow this dazzling terminology.

3

THE USES OF 'INTUITION'

If literary excellence is to be judged by reference to some intelligible standard, some set of rules which all can understand—and attempts have often been made to frame such rules—then it should be possible to set them out and explain on what principles they are based; for excellence must be related to some need, some function. If a thing is said to be 'good', then it must be good for some purpose. In particular, if art is to be judged good or bad, then we ought to be able to say what it can be good for. The natural answer would be, of course, that art gives pleasure, and that therefore that art is best which gives most pleasure. The question then remains: do we count heads or measure the degree of emotion? Many professional critics of art and poetry would accept neither of these criteria. They believe that in relation to all forms of art there are certain absolute values that cannot be referred to any special function or measured against any general criterion, and that of these we have, or some of us have, a direct 'intuitive' knowledge. In that case our standard must be our own or somebody else's intuition. Either we must suppose that every man's intuition reveals the same standard, in which case we should all agree as to what is good in art and what is bad—and that is manifestly not the case—or we must resign ourselves to the existence of a number of different and independent standards. The solution of this dilemma seems usually to be that some people have a higher standard than others, so that before we can determine the excellence of a work of art we have to determine the comparative elevation of the various standards.

The Everyman edition of Coleridge's *Biographia Literaria* has an Introduction by Arthur Symons who quotes some lines from Shelley on Coleridge and says that they "are not merely good criticism, they are final; they leave nothing more to be said. Criticism at such a height is no longer mere reasoning; it has the absolute sanction of intuition" (p. x). This "absolute sanction" is commonly invoked by critics—though not always quite so bluntly—to vindicate their personal taste. The use of the word 'intuition' here must mean that, in the opinion of Mr. Symons, Shelley did not need to use his reasoning faculty in order to pass judgment on Coleridge, but was able to arrive directly at his estimate. To have an intuition that it is going to rain or that one is going to win a sweepstake means that one has some kind of direct knowledge of the future or of something of which one could not have any knowledge by such normal methods as inquiry, experiment, or reasoning. Many animals have but limited powers of reasoning, and some benefit little from experience. They do not make conscious inferences from the data presented to them, they judge by instinct, as we say. Birds and fishes find their way on their migrations, and insects can sometimes anticipate the weather. Fabre tells that the Processionary caterpillar does not go out on its nocturnal foray when the weather is going to be bad. From the conditions which prevail in the early evening it knows what they will be later in the night. We do not know what senses these animals depend on for these purposes, but no biologist would accept as an explanation that they possess supernatural powers. Something in the state of the atmosphere when a storm approaches *informs* the caterpillar of what is coming, or rather *excites* him to perform the appropriate action. A certain complex situation leads to a definite and appropriate action. Similarly some people can recognise footsteps or distinguish different vintages of wine without depending on any conscious inference. It is in such cases that we speak of 'intuition'.

Intuition is discussed at considerable length by Benedetto Croce in his *Aesthetic*, and I shall devote the rest of this chapter to a critique of his views. The full title of the English translation by Douglas Ainslie (from which I have taken the passages quoted) is *Aesthetic as Science of Expression and*

General Linguistic (London: Macmillan, 1909). We read on the first page:

> In ordinary life, constant appeal is made to intuitive knowledge. It is said to be impossible to give expression to certain truths; that they are not demonstrable by syllogisms; that they must be learned intuitively. The politician finds fault with the abstract reasoner, who is without a lively knowledge of actual conditions, the pedagogue insists on the necessity of developing the intuitive faculty in the pupil before everything else; the critic in judging a work of art makes it a point of honour to set aside theory and abstractions, and to judge it by direct intuition; the practical man professes to live rather by intuition than by reason.

These statements are plausible so far as the negative side is concerned. The philosopher, psychologist, literary theorist, who are nothing if not abstract reasoners, do often exhibit a certain ignorance of "actual conditions", and this is just where 'intuition' appears to come to their aid.

Croce goes on to speak of a science of intuitive knowledge and a science of intellective knowledge, and he appears to assume that they are two distinct species. The view that there are two faculties, intellection (or reason) and intuition, both of which acquaint us with the truth but in different ways, may well be encouraged by the basis it seems to provide for attractive theories about religion, ethics, and art. In this book Croce is primarily concerned with the last, and he maintains that intuition is the foundation of art, and that philosophers deal in reasoning and concepts.

Croce does not restrict the meaning of the word 'intuition' to the perception of the actual. It is true, he says, that perception is intuition, but intuition is not always perception. He distinguishes between the image formed as the direct result of some sensory impression, the image, for example, of the room in which he is actually sitting, and the image which is formed of some remote past or merely possible situation. He says that the child is unable to distinguish the true from the false, history from fable, and he thinks that this gives us the idea of the nature of intuition. He says that "Intuition is the undifferentiated unity of the perception of the real and of the simple image of the possible" (p. 6). He seems to mean that intuition is something which combines the virtues of perception and imagination. He adds that there are intuitions with which space and time have nothing to do; intuitions such as "a tint of sky and a tint of sentiment, an 'Ah!' of pain and an effort of will, objectified in consciousness". Again:

> That which intuition reveals in a work of art is not space and time, but character, individual physiognomy. (p. 7)

One thing is already fairly clear, and that is that Croce takes 'intuition' to be, not a *word* in need of definition but a *thing* to be investigated. But he does not explain what he wishes us to understand by this thing. How can we be aware of a tint of sky except in relation to some real situation, observed or recalled or imagined? How can we have a feeling of pain which is not situated somewhere in the body? How can we be conscious of an effort of will except in relation to some situation that concerns us in space and time? He insists that in order to discover the intuition we must make complete abstraction of all these *concepts*; "spatiality" and "temporality" may be "fused with the intuition" but they are not part of it. When we listen to a story or a piece of music we are not, according to him, conscious of temporal sequence. He could say in the same way that when we read a book we are not conscious of the letters and the printing, or even of the individual words; and when the pianist performs he is not conscious of his fingers or of the keyboard. This, of course, is only partly true, but it is impossible to discuss the matter until we have agreed about what is conscious and what is not. He goes on to claim to have "freed intuitive knowledge from any suggestion of intellectualism" (p. 8), although he has not as yet given any intelligible psychological account of what is to be understood by either of these words.

If intuitive knowledge is as genuine a form of knowledge as the intellectual variety, it will not be hard to show that the artist is just as important a person as the scientist. Croce objects to the view "that art is not knowledge, that it does not tell the truth, that it does not belong to the world of theory, but to the world of feeling". These statements, he says, arise from the failure to realize exactly the theoretic character of the simple intuition . . . . We have seen that intuition is knowledge, free of concepts and more simple than the so-called perception of the real. Since art is knowledge and form, it does not belong to the world of feeling and of psychic material. (p. 29)

So the artist is not simply telling us what he feels like. He has something to tell us about the world which is of vital importance. He does not give us scientific information, but reveals to us the world as it is, undistorted by concepts, or by intellection.

Croce thinks that you cannot have a genuine intuition without expressing it. "Intuitive activity possesses intuitions to the extent that it expresses them" (p. 13). Of course, expression does not mean only verbal expression. It may be "pictorial, or verbal, or musical" or even something else, but there must always be "expression of some kind: . . . to no intuition can expression be wanting, because it is an inseparable part of intuition" (pp. 13–14). He seems to suppose that we cannot have an idea without expressing it. We cannot

possess a true intuition of a geometrical figure, unless we possess so accurate an image of it as to be able to trace it immediately upon paper or on a slate. (p. 14)

Apparently we have to include in the idea of expression the simple capacity to express. Even so, this principle is hard to accept. Can we not have a true intuition of our friend's face, of the street in which we live, of our dog, and even of ourselves? Yet there are many of us who cannot trace any of these things immediately upon either paper or slate. If this power of expression is an essential of all intuitions, then many people must have but few.

Admitting that his proposition may seem paradoxical, he goes on to explain that we often suppose we have a more complete intuition of reality than we really have:

One often hears people say that they have in their minds many important thoughts, but that they are not able to express them. In truth, if they really had them, they would have coined them into beautiful, ringing words, and thus expressed them. (pp. 14–15)

So that intuitions always can and usually do express themselves, otherwise they are not intuitions.

Croce thinks, very naturally, that most of us have but
very inadequate intuitions, though we do not realise how inadequate they are. It must be remembered that for him intuition includes perception and imagination and expression. We
suppose, he says, that we could imagine a Madonna of
Raphael and only lack the technical skill to paint it. That, he
says, is an error, for if we could really imagine it we could
also paint it. He then enlarges on the narrow range of the ordinary man's intuitions; and he compares our mental
representations of things to the index of a book, where "the
labels tied to things take the place of the things themselves"
(p. 16). This is true enough if he means that in the course of
our reflections we form a very sketchy image of the thing we
are considering, often no more than the word which stands
for it. This verbal thinking is only too evident in Croce
himself. But it is wrong to say that we cannot have a clear and
vivid idea without being able to express it adequately. We
may witness a most striking event in real life which brands
itself on our memory, and yet be unable to reproduce it either
in words or pictures.

Croce seems not to realize that his illustrations do not illustrate his propositions. Speaking of painting, he says:

> It has been observed by those who have best studied the psychology
> of artists, that when, after having given a rapid glance at anyone, they
> attempt to obtain a true intuition of him, in order, for example, to
> paint his portrait, then this ordinary vision, that seemed so precise, so
> lively, reveals itself as little better than nothing. What remains is
> found to be at the most some superficial trait, which would not even
> suffice for a caricature. The person to be painted stands before the
> artist like a world to discover. Michel Angelo said, 'one paints, not
> with one's hands, but with one's brain'. Leonardo shocked the prior
> of the Convent delle Grazie by standing for days together opposite
> the 'Last Supper' without touching it with the brush. He remarked of
> this attitude 'that men of the most lofty genius, when they are doing
> the least work, are then the most active, seeking invention with their
> minds'. (pp. 16–17)

So in order to obtain an adequate intuition one has to do a
great deal of thinking. Croce seems not to notice any difficulty here. We have to suppose that Leonardo, gazing for days

on end at his unfinished picture, was not engaged in exercising his 'intellectual function'. How Croce can be quite sure of this is hard to understand.

The first chapter ends with the assertion that intuition is in fact nothing more nor less than expression (p. 19). In the course of his discussion of 'expression' Croce asks whether a book can be "well thought and badly written", and decides that this is impossible (p. 40). It is true that a man cannot be expected to write clearly if his thoughts are muddled. (This much is clear from Croce's own writings.) The written expression can hardly be clearer than the ideas to be expressed. But the converse does not follow. A skilled artificer may have a clear idea of how to do a certain piece of work and yet be at a loss to describe the operation in words so that one ignorant of the craft can understand. A certain skill in the use of words is needed besides a clear idea of the process. But for Croce there were perhaps not many ideas connected with art and philosophy which did not consist almost exclusively of words, and in that case it does indeed follow that word and idea correspond. Insofar as an idea consists in a verbal formula it is clear that it can always be expressed by uttering the words of which it is composed. He has perhaps overlooked the difference between the memory of passive sensations and the memory of our own actions, which include speech. Speaking is an action which we can revive and rehearse in the imagination, and the act itself can be repeated when we will. Seeing and hearing are not acts in the same way and it is certain that we cannot see and hear at will whatever we wish. We can recall sights and sounds in our imagination more or less clearly according to the quality of our memory, but unless this recall is itself to be called *expression*, the clearness of our idea does not suffice to ensure that we can express it.

Croce goes on to admit that "sometimes we possess thoughts (concepts) in an intuitive form, or in an abbreviated or, better, peculiar expression, sufficient for us, but not sufficient to communicate it with ease to another or other definite individuals" (p. 40). In view of the fundamental opposition between concept and intuition expounded in a previous chapter we are surprised to learn that a concept may be possessed in an intuitive form. He is evidently thinking here of verbal expression, for this is the normal method of expressing our thoughts to one another. He knows that he is often unable to convey his ideas to other people; he can hardly have failed to realise this whenever he found himself in the society of unsympathetic listeners. He does not conclude that there may be something amiss with his ideas, but believes that he can express them to himself by making use of an abbreviated or peculiar expression which happens not to be suited to the understanding of his hearers:

> Hence people say, inaccurately, that we have the thought without the expression; whereas it should properly be said that we have, indeed, the expression, but in a form that is not easy of social communication. (p. 40)

In more naive language this experience is sometimes expressed by the formula: 'I know what I mean, but I can't put it into words'. Everyone knows that this often signifies that the speaker does not know what he means. However, Croce goes on to say that this peculiar or abbreviated expression is not to be regarded as entirely useless for social communication. There are some who prefer it and who "would be displeased with the greater development of it, necessary for other people" (p. 40). In its abbreviated form it is often more impressive than when it is 'developed'. Those who like a touch of mystery, and who believe that the deeper thoughts are of necessity a little obscure, feel more at home with elliptical, metaphorical, and abstract statements, which, incidentally, are less exposed to criticism and contradiction and emotionally more satisfying. Oracles have always avoided plain speaking and the policy has generally been found profitable.

Croce next speaks of "literary mediocrity" and says that we may pardon mediocre expression in "thinkers and men of science", but not in "pure artists":

> The poet or painter who lacks form, lacks everything, because he lacks *himself*. Poetical material permeates the Soul of all: the expression alone, that is to say the form, makes the poet. And here appears the truth of the thesis which denies to art all content, as content being understood just the intellectual concept. In this sense, when we take 'content' as equal to 'concept' it is most true, not only that art does not consist of content, but also that *it has no content*. (p. 42)

The scientist has something to say, and so long as he makes his meaning clear we can tolerate a certain want of elegance in his style. But the artist has nothing to offer except the charm of his manner, so we expect more of him in this respect. That appears to be the meaning of the passage, although the argument is obscure. "Poetical material permeates the Soul of all." Perhaps he means that anything is potential material for the poet. This, of course, is a modern idea. "The poet . . . lacks everything, because he lacks himself" is a difficult saying. How does one lack oneself? "When we take 'content' as equal to 'concept' it is most true . . . that art . . . has no content." One might have thought that it would have been better to say simply that art has no concept. But this would not even appear to convey anything, and so the proposition remains: 'Art has no content'. He adds that, by contrast with art, history *is* content (p. 44). History "is not form", yet

> . . . as form, it is nothing but intuition or aesthetic fact. History does not seek for laws nor form concepts; it employs neither induction nor deduction; it is directed *ad narrandum, non ad demonstrandum*; it does not construct universals and abstractions but posits intuitions. The this, the that, the *individuum omni modo determinatum*, is its kingdom, as it is the kingdom of art. History, therefore, is included under the universal concept of art.

History is not form, nevertheless *as* form it is intuition; and intuition, as we have been told, *is* form (pp. 26, 29). At the same time history is content, and content is concept (p. 29). Yet history does not form concepts but posits intuitions. Moreover history *is* intuition. If in all this there are no contradictions it is because the words are without meaning. With this kind of writing Croce fills a number of books on literature, history, and philosophy and has gained a reputation for deep understanding.

As we have seen (above, p. 32), intuition commonly means some capacity to obtain knowledge without the aid of any process of inference. But such immediate understanding occurs again and again in cases of perception, and no one supposes that anything mysterious is involved. When we see the face of a familiar friend, we know immediately who it is. When we smell a certain acrid odour we know at once that something is burning. Certain other smells impossible to describe in any other way inform us at once of the presence of fish, onions, petrol, turpentine, alcohol, or beer.

What is this process of recognition? When a certain smell informs us that there is an onion close at hand, what does the information actually consist in? The smell is linked in our brain to a whole collection of memories, visual, gustatory, tactile, and so on, simple and complex, and when our olfactory organ is excited by this particular effluvium this complex of memories is excited. We do not and cannot recall all our past experiences of onions in a moment of time. We may, in the course of a few seconds or even minutes, revive some of them. What seems to happen is rather that the whole collection is partially mobilised so that they are more ready to be recalled than they would otherwise have been, and some action related to onions may occur. It may be no more than the remark: 'I smell onions'. Instead of an action there may be merely a getting ready for action, a bracing of the system so as to be ready to deal with onions should they take a more prominent position in the situation. Thus if the waiter is approaching with a dish of onions we may form an instantaneous resolution to say 'No, thank you', when we feel him leaning over us. The action is postponed until the dish has been thrust under our nose, but it has been prepared ever since the dish came into the room. This attitude which precedes action, and which may resolve itself in different ways according to subsequent events, may be described as a physiological response to onions, and in some cases it may be a very vigorous response even though no outward movement betrays its existence.

What happens when there is an inference and a 'rational' process? We start with a sensation. This gives rise to an idea, which may arise immediately or may take a long time to be excited, if any great number of the memories of which it is composed have to pass into consciousness. Reaction to the situation may occur immediately in the former case, or at any stage in the process of protracted recall. When reaction is rapid, people are accustomed to use the word 'intuition', especially when they do not understand the linkage involved, when the power of recognising the situation seems incomprehensible to them. When the reaction is slow and preceded by a period of hesitation and reflection, they talk of intellectual processes or reasoning. But the distinction as it is generally made is fallacious.

Commentators on Croce have done little to make his ideas clear. Wimsatt and Brooks discuss his views in their *Literary Criticism: A Short History*, to which I have referred in the previous chapter. Concerning his overall philosophic system, they suggest that he was not satisfied with the theory of Marx but, as he had a hankering after Hegel, wanted a theory which was at least as Hegelian as that of Marx:

> In the Hegelian idealism there was something, a world or nature on which spirit worked in a dialectical process. Marxism reduced this to a very thoroughly monistic working of material nature in and through itself. Croce, using as his entrance into the metaphysical realm no other than a literary observation, concerning the breakdown of classical rules and genres of art, arrives at an opposite, but equally thoroughgoing monism of spirit. (p. 501)

We are presumably to take this to mean a thoroughly monistic working of spirit 'in and through itself'. As to how Croce gained entrance to the metaphysical realm by means of a literary observation, our two authors say:

> His criticism of the classical genres . . . enabled him to lay his finger 'on the point at which "nature", the product of man's own spirit, is introduced into the pure spiritual world of art.' Having 'thus denied the reality of nature in art', he was led by degrees 'to deny it everywhere and to discover everywhere its true character, not as reality but as the product of abstracting thought'. 'Spirit' in the Crocean philosophy is the 'absolute reality'. Spirit 'generates the contents of experience'.

This sounds rather like Leibniz's theory of pre-established harmony, the whole universe being presented to the individual soul not as a result of the effects produced by the universe but as a kind of spontaneous internal illusion in the soul which develops in consequence of its own internal machinery.[1] The chief difference seems to be that in Croce's view there is nothing outside the mind. To avoid what Wimsatt and Brooks call the "embarrassments" that follow from such a view, Croce does not speak of *the* soul, but of

"spirit", without any article. But if our two authors are to be
trusted, he did not feel this embarrassment very much, for
they go on:

> Some of these contents of experience, it is true, assume the character
> (by abstraction) of something external to the knowing spirit and . . .
> even become the means by which further acts of spirit are projected
> and made known to individual spiritual agents external to each other
> and to the immediate consciousness which we must suppose to be
> spirit for the philosopher of the system.

The "philosopher of the system" is presumably Croce
himself. It seems to be implied that the "immediate consciousness" is spirit for him, but not for anyone else. That
some of the contents of experience should assume the
character of something external to the knowing spirit is in accordance with the theory of Leibniz. But the projection of
acts of spirit onto other spiritual agents external to each other
(i.e. onto other people) is something Leibniz seems not to
have thought of.

Wimsatt and Brooks go on to make certain respectful
criticisms of Croce, but what they do not do is explain the
psychological process by which a man supposes himself to be
thinking when he is merely making up sentences. As they do
this themselves they are, perhaps, not in a good position to
criticise this failing. It is hard to see any value in works of art
if they, like the rest of the world in which we live, have no
'reality' and are merely projections of Croce's mind or of
'spirit'. So they complain that "the Crocean system"

> has contributed its influence to the sway of critical impressionism. By
> the mere fact that it is a form of monistic expressionism and idealism,
> it has tended to undercut the notion of real values and hence to
> remove the background against which even an idealistic theory of art
> values must make its claims. (p. 518)

In this kind of picturesque writing abstractions become as
real and personal as the characters in Bunyan's *Pilgrim's Progress*. *Theories* make claims as if they were in a law-court or
an insurance office; the *notion* of real values is undercut like
the price of bacon, and the *system* removes the background
like a common stage hand.

PART TWO

VERBIAGE
AND RELIGION

4

KANT AS
DEFENDER OF THE FAITH

In the early eighteenth century the arguments of Christian apologists appealed to reason even when they emphasized the insufficient powers of the human mind. Joseph Butler, for instance, argued in his *The Analogy of Religion* (1736) that the 'difficulties' which we meet in religion are no greater than those which perplex the study of nature. He never suggested that the limitations of reason can be compensated by the exercise of some other faculty for ascertaining truth. Reason relies on experience, and in all his arguments Butler claimed to do the same.

Hume, Voltaire, and others put an end to this comfortable state of mind. By the mid-nineteenth century things were going from bad to worse, and J. H. Newman was feeling thoroughly miserable. He wrote in 1840:

> I expect a great attack upon the Bible—indeed I have long expected it. At the present moment indications of what is coming gather. Those wretched Socialists on the one hand, then Carlyle on the other. . . . I had hoped he might have come round right, for it was easy to see he was not a believer; but they say he is settled the wrong way. His view is that Christianity has good in it, or is good *as far as it goes*, which, when applied to Scripture, is, of course, a picking and choosing of its contents. Then, again, you have Arnold's school, such as it is (I do hope he will be frightened back), giving up the inspiration of the Old Testament, or of all Scripture (I do not say Arnold himself does). Then you have Milman, clenching his 'History of the Jews' by a 'History of Christianity' which they say is worse; and just in the same line. Then you have all your political economists who cannot accept (it is impossible) the Scripture rules about alms-giving, renunciation of wealth, self-denial, etc., and then your geologists, giving up parts of the Old Testament. All these and many more spirits seem uniting and forming into something shocking.[1]

Six years later appeared George Eliot's translation of Strauss's *Leben Jesu*. In 1859 came the *Origin of Species*, in 1863 Lyell's *Antiquity of Man*, and about the same time Bishop Colenso's commentaries on the Pentateuch. Where-ever men undertook to make investigations with the light of reason, they seemed to stumble on something disturbing.

At first defence consisted in a denial of the new doctrines, and insistence on the wickedness of doubt and the perils of incredulity. But the material achievements of science tended to establish the authority of the scientists, and the lectures and writings of Huxley, Tyndall, and Clifford reached a wide public. Meanwhile the intelligible philosophers seemed all to be on the side of the infidels—Comte, Mill, Spencer, and the historian of philosophy, Lewes. It was in this predicament that Kant and Hegel were first invoked in this country.

Coleridge effected Kant's introduction. He wrote in his *Biographia Literaria*, 1817, of the "illustrious sage of Königsberg", of the "originality, the depth and the compression" of his thoughts, of his "adamantine chain of logic". He claimed to be still reading Kant's books "with undiminished delight and increasing admiration" after fifteen years of familiarity with them. That there was some difficulty in understanding the philosopher's meaning Coleridge admits. "An idea", he says, "in the highest sense of that word, cannot be conveyed but by a symbol. . . . And for those who could not pierce through this symbolic husk, his writings were not intended." But this want of perfect clearness Coleridge ascribes to a necessary precaution, since Kant, he believes, was in danger of persecution. "Questions which cannot be fully answered without exposing the respondent to personal danger are not entitled to a fair answer."

Coleridge's attitude was not initially shared by other English writers. De Quincey, for instance, ridiculed Kant's style, comparing a typical sentence of the *Kritik der reinen Vernunft* (*Critique of Pure Reason*) to an old family coach packed full to capacity: "Everything that could ever be needed in the way of explanation, illustration, restraint, inference, by clause or indirect comment, was to be crammed, according to this philosopher's taste, into the front pockets, side pockets or rear pockets of the one original sentence.''[2] Carlyle was even more severely critical, and wrote in his diary in 1823:

> Kant's philosophy has a gigantic appearance at a distance, enveloped in clouds and darkness, shadowed forth in types and symbols of unknown and fantastic derivation. There is an apparatus, and a flourishing of drums and trumpets, and a tumultuous *Marktschreyerei*, as if all the earth were going to renew its youth; and the Esoterics are equally allured by all this pomp and circumstance, and repelled by the hollowness and airy nothingness of the ware which is presented to them. Any of the results which have been made intelligible to us turn out to be—like Dryden in the 'Battle of the Books'—a helmet of rusty iron large as a kitchen pot, and within it a head little bigger than a nut.[3]

A few years later, in the state of extreme agitation which preceded his wedding, he tried to calm his nerves by reading the *Kritik*. He had reached the 150th page "when he found that it was too abstruse for his condition, and that Scott's novels would answer better".[4] He also refers to Kant in his *Life of Schiller*, published in 1825, where he writes in Part 3:

> The air of mysticism connected with these doctrines was attractive to the German mind, with which the vague and the vast are always pleasing qualities; the dreadful array of first principles, the forest huge of terminology and definitions . . . seemed sublime rather than appalling to the Germans; men who shrink not at toil, and to whom a certain degree of darkness appears a native element, essential for giving play to that deep meditative enthusiasm which forms so important a feature in their character.

The attempt to *read* Kant, to which I have referred, came in 1826, *after* these expressions of opinion. Whether he ever succeeded in getting through the *Kritik der reinen Vernunft* does not appear, but he soon after changed his view about the transcendental philosophy. He had evidently discovered that the practical effect of the new doctrine was to rehabilitate some of the values called in question by eighteenth-century writers. For 'Englightenment', 'Voltairism', and 'Encyclopaedism', Carlyle had a natural repugnance, and his conversion to Kantism may possibly have been the result of discovering that it was regarded as an antidote to these poisons. At all events, in his essay on the 'State of German Literature' which appeared in 1827, he writes in a different vein. It is fairly obvious that he is still describing the doctrines at second hand. He refers to the belief then current in England and previously, as we saw, shared by himself, that Kant, Fichte, and Schelling were mystics. He seeks to correct such a wrong impression, and calls Kant

> A quiet, vigilant, clear-sighted man, who had become distinguished to the world in mathematics before he attempted philosophy; who in his writings generally, on this and other subjects, is perhaps characterised by no quality so much as precisely by the distinctness of his conceptions, and the sequence and iron strictness with which he reasons .... Right or wrong as his hypothesis may be, no one that knows him will suspect that he himself had not seen it, and seen over it; had not meditated it with calmness and deep thought, and studied throughout to expound it with scientific rigour.[5]

Exactly what is involved in seeing and seeing over a hypothesis, right or wrong, the reader is left to guess. But calm and depth and scientific rigour are qualities that command respect. As if to remove any doubt in the reader's mind, Carlyle adds that the *Kritik der reinen Vernunft* is not an unduly difficult book:

> It is true, there is an unknown and forbidding terminology to be mastered; but is not this the case also with Chemistry, and Astronomy, and all other Sciences that deserve the name of science? It is true, a careless or unprepared reader will find Kant's writing a riddle; but will a reader of this sort make much of Newton's *Principia*, or D'Alembert's *Calculus of Variations*?

His readers would perhaps have preferred to hear some account of Kant's actual investigations and discoveries, but it is suggested to them that such matters cannot be briefly summarised. They must first master the "forbidding terminology"—they are not told how; since there were no textbooks, it would be a difficult task—and then undertake for themselves the study of a philosophy, compared with which physics and mathematics are, he says, "plain subjects". The readers of the *Edinburgh Review* would perhaps decide that this is not a matter on which they would like to trust to their own judgement, and be content to accept the word of the learned reviewer:

> Kant, Fichte and Schelling, are men of cool judgment, and determinate energetic character; men of science and profound and universal investigation; nowhere does the world, in all its bearings, spiritual

or material, theoretic or practical, lie pictured in clearer or truer colours than in such heads as these (vol. cit., pp. 64–65).

Why this enthusiasm for the transcendental philosophy? Had Carlyle made himself familiar with the terminology of this master science, and assimilated it, as he had previously assimilated Newton and D'Alembert? Possibly. But it is not necessary to assume this. In his essay he goes on to give the gist of the new philosophy. He first recalls the effect of Hume:

> British philosophy, since the time of Hume, appears to them [the Germans] nothing more than a "laborious and unsuccessful striving to build dike after dike in front of our Churches and Judgment-halls, and so turn back from them the deluge of Scepticism, with which that extraordinary writer overflowed us, and still threatens to destroy whatever we value most." This is A. W. Schlegel's verdict; given in words equivalent to these (vol. cit., p. 68).

It seems that Carlyle, since his first unsuccessful attempt to understand what the *Kritik der reinen Vernunft* was about, has learned—perhaps from Schlegel—that it was a new and highly effectual defence of "whatever we value most": that is to say, our religious beliefs. With this clue he seems to have tried again, and this time found little difficulty in extracting the kernel of the matter, which he describes as follows:

> The Germans . . . deny . . . that Sense is the only inlet of Knowledge, that Experience is the primary ground of Belief. Their Primitive Truth, however, they seek, not historically and by experiment, in the universal persuasions of men, but by intuition, in the deepest and purest nature of Man. Instead of attempting, which they consider vain, to prove the existence of God, Virtue, an immaterial Soul, by inferences drawn, as the conclusion of all Philosophy, from the world of Sense, they find these things written as the beginning of all philosophy, in obscured but ineffaceable characters, within our inmost being; and themselves first affording any certainty and clear meaning to that very world of Sense, by which we endeavour to demonstrate them. God *is*, nay alone *is*, for with like emphasis we cannot say that anything else is. This is the Absolute, the Primitively True, which the philosopher seeks. Endeavouring by logical argument to prove the existence of God, a Kantist might say, would be like taking out a candle to look for the sun; nay, gaze steadily into your candle-light, and the sun himself may be invisible. To open the inward eye to the sight of this Primitively True; or rather we might call it, to clear off the Obscurations of Sense, which eclipse this truth within us, so that we may see it, and believe it not only to be true, but

the foundation and essence of all other truth—may, in such language as we are here using, be said to be the problem of Critical Philosophy. (vol. cit., pp. 68–69)

It is already evident that Kant has thrown up a formidable dike against the floods of scepticism. How was it accomplished? Very simply, by discovering the difference between the 'Reason' and the 'Understanding', which, Carlyle explains, are "organs or rather . . . modes of operation by which the mind discovers truth":

Reason, the Kantists say, is of a higher nature than Understanding . . . . Reason discerns Truth itself, the absolutely and primitively *True*; while Understanding discerns only *relations*, and cannot decide without *if*. The proper province of Understanding is all, strictly speaking, *real*, practical and material knowledge, Mathematics, Physics, Political Economy, the adaptation of means to ends in the whole business of life. . . . Let it not step beyond this province, however, not usurp the province of Reason, which it is appointed to obey, and cannot rule over without ruin to the whole spiritual man. Should Understanding attempt to prove the existence of God, it ends, if thorough-going and consistent with itself, in Atheism, or a faint possible Theism, which scarcely differs from this: should it speculate of Virtue, it ends in *Utility*, making Prudence and a sufficiently cunning love of Self the highest good. Consult Understanding about the Beauty of Poetry, and it asks, Where is this Beauty? or discovers it at length in rhythms and fitnesses, and male and female rhymes. Witness also its everlasting paradoxes on Necessity and the Freedom of the Will; its ominous silence on the end and meaning of man; and the enigma which, under such inspection, the whole purport of existence becomes. (vol. cit., pp. 69–70)

The 'mode of operation' has become a kind of evil counsellor, an impostor that arrogates to himself powers and functions rightly reserved for a higher being. At this point in his essay the rhapsodist seems to have felt some slight scruples, for he continues:

Will the Kantists forgive us for the loose and popular manner in which we must here speak of these things, to bring them in any measure before the eyes of our readers?

The Kantists would indeed be ungrateful to object, since this is the kind of advertisement which counts. It may seem a little overdone; and the more intelligent reader might feel curious about the reasoning process by which such reassuring results had been reached. How had these German philosophers discovered this faculty of 'Reason', hitherto so unaccountably overlooked? If the floods of scepticism were to be more effectually dammed by these new dikes, then it must be because of some infallibility in the manner of their construction, some secret which Carlyle could not reveal without abandoning the 'loose and popular manner'. For, with as good grounds as he has shown for this new and convenient psychology, one might as easily establish the existence of a score of independent 'faculties' for discovering truth. Why just two 'modes of operation'? Why only the Reason and the Understanding? Why not also the Intellect, the Judgement, the Intelligence, the Wits, the Sagacity, the Discernment, the Insight, the Soul, the Spirit, the Mind, the Genius, the Gumption? Since the considerations which led Kant to decide on these two operations are not mentioned, or even hinted at, the reader might be excused for wondering whether the new panacea was really any more reliable than the old, in spite of what was claimed for it.

The story of Carlyle's conversion to Kant is, then, quite simple. At first he was repelled by the unintelligible jargon. Later he heard the philosopher well spoken of by respectable Germans and quotes, for instance, Schlegel's comment that "in respect of its probable influence on the moral culture of Europe", Kant's philosophy "stands on a line with the Reformation" (vol. cit., p. 66). From such hints he learned that the practical effect of the new doctrine was to rehabilitate some of the values called in question by earlier eighteenth-century writers. He therefore welcomed an ally and was prepared to assume that Kant's obscurity was due to his profundity. It is plain that he never tried very hard to understand the *Kritik*. Nothing in his exposition suggests a serious study.[6]

Carlyle, we saw, suggests that the difficulty the reader finds in reading the *Kritik* is comparable to what we would meet with in a treatise of mathematics. But is this comparison really just? A work on the higher mathematics assumes of necessity a knowledge of the lower, and algebra presupposes elementary arithmetic. No amount of study and concentration would enable one ignorant of the elements to master a more advanced work. Nobody can divine the meaning of an unfamiliar mathematical symbol. He must go back to the definition, and if this is given in unfamiliar terms he must seek the definition of the latter, which will probably be supplied only in a more elementary work. But if the student starts at the beginning and progresses gradually, he can in time understand the more abstruse works. Now Kant's book is not difficult in this sense at all. Mathematical symbols have a quite definite meaning, but the words used by Kant have not. The former are, to the uninitiated, unintelligible, but the latter are, to a great extent, familiar. But this familiarity does not help. Such words as *sensation, perception, understanding* are familiar enough, but their meaning depends largely on their context. In an intelligible context we can understand them. In the dictionary their meaning must always be illustrated by an example of their actual use in a hypothetical context. And such words as these have a very variable meaning. One may explain the meaning of the word *earwig* by producing a specimen of the species. One can in a similar way define such words as *heart* or *brain*, although it may not be so easy to produce a specimen. But when we seek a definition of *thought, understanding*, and other psychological terms, this method is not available. When a psychologist defines such things he is merely stating his own theory. Kant cheerfully invents a faculty such as 'pure intuition *a priori*' (reine Anschauung *a priori*) and then speaks of it as if it were among the accepted notions of all psychologists and philosophers. His analysis of the mind is fantastic, and the great difficulty in reading him is in reconstructing this Kantian conception of mind. The whole elaborate apparatus of faculties into which he divides the human mind has no relation to any physiological or psychological facts, and has never been made use of for any scientific psychological purpose.

In Paragraph 41 of his *Prolegomena* (1783) Kant draws attention to his own merit in having made the distinction between Reason and Understanding; and he holds that, while it is the function of the Understanding to supply information about things which depend for their existence on various conditions, the Reason is not satisfied with this and seeks knowledge of the unconditioned. The Understanding can enable us to experience things, but the Reason desires information about the unconditioned soul, or free self, the unconditioned world (the absolute whole of all possible experience), and the unconditioned entity we call God. Our ideas of these entities are not derived from experience, and Kant supposes that they are simply innate in the Reason (Paragraph 40). But they can never be confirmed nor refuted by experience (Paragraph 42). This last is very important. There would be little objection to confirmation, except that the possibility would seem to imply the opposite possibility of confutation, and so it is as well to be explicit about the latter. What the philosopher asserts on the strength of what his Reason tells him cannot be invalidated by what the scientist may say on the strength of what he learns from his Understanding. In the next paragraph Kant again stresses his own great merit in having made this discovery about distinct faculties, and contrasts himself with lesser folk who indulge in "mere rhapsodising". However, in fixing the limits of pure Reason, Kant points out that we cannot altogether avoid looking over the fence. Reason, he says (Paragraph 57) cannot *know* God, but must posit him, because it can never rest satisfied with explaining one thing in terms of another (which is all that Understanding can accomplish). In the discussion that follows, he admits that when we try to endow the idea of a supreme being with definite characteristics, we must derive these from experience. But he supposes that when we posit merely a supreme being, without any kind of details, we remain unassailable. He means that the pure idea entertained by the Reason is an idea without any thinkable content. This kind of abstraction was very familiar to Kant. The really important thing about his philosophy was felt to be that it provides a crushing reply to Hume's scepticism and to all forms of unbelief. And the special virtue of his answer to scepticism is that, instead of trying to meet the sceptic on his own ground, with rational and intelligible arguments, the new tactic consists in a denial of the validity of logic and argument.

The seed sown by Carlyle took some time to germinate. Sir William Hamilton seems to have adopted the transcendental spirit without acknowledging himself a Kantist. And it was this spirit which Mill attacked. Mill speaks of the two rival philosophies, "that of Intuition, and that of Experience and Association", and says that he had at first thought that Sir William Hamilton occupied "a kind of intermediate position" between them. But Hamilton's "Lectures and the Dissertations on Reid dispelled this illusion".[7] Mill became, of course, the chief enemy of the transcendentalists. He was evidently endowed with much Understanding and very little Reason. His mind was of a lower order, adapted only for the province of 'practical and material knowledge'—Logic, for example, and Political Economy—and lacked the superior subtlety, and that 'far finer culture' by which the Reason is enabled to 'discern Truth itself, the absolutely and primitively True'. For Mill, the difference between the two schools of philosophy was not merely a matter of "abstract speculation". He found that it was "full of practical consequence", and lay "at the foundation of all the greatest differences of practical opinion in an age of progress". He says:

> The practical reformer has continually to demand that changes be made in things which are supported by powerful and widely-spread feelings, or to question the apparent necessity and indefeasibleness of established facts; and it is often an indispensable part of his argument to show how those powerful feelings had their origin, and how those facts came to seem necessary and indefeasible. There is therefore a natural hostility between him and a philosophy which discourages the explanation of feelings and moral facts by circumstances and association, and prefers to treat them as ultimate elements of human nature; a philosophy which is addicted to holding up favourite doctrines as intuitive truths, and deems intuition to be the voice of Nature and God, speaking with an authority higher than that of reason.[8]

In the same year in which appeared Mill's *Examination of Sir William Hamilton's Philosophy*, there was also published *The Secret of Hegel* by J. H. Stirling.[9] In the Preface, Stirling says that "if it is true . . . that the thoughts of German Philosophy are not yet adequately turned to account, but remain as yet almost, as it were, beyond the reach whether of friend or foe, there must be some unusual difficulty of intelligence in the case'' (pp. xxxvii–xxxviii). He then explains the source of this difficulty in terms equally in need of explanation, but ends with words similar to those earlier used by Carlyle: ''. . . The difficulties of Hegel are simply technical, and . . . his *Logic* is to be read only by such means as will enable us to read the *Principia* of Newton—industry, tenacity, perseverance'' (p. liii). In those days Newton seems to have been regarded as the ideal example of an incredibily abstruse author whose authority, nevertheless, nobody seemed inclined to question; in our day his place has been taken by Einstein.

Now if anybody will take the trouble to examine *The Secret of Hegel* for himself, he will find some parts of the Preface, at least, not difficult to understand. But when he comes to what may be presumed to be the principal analysis, he will be fortunate indeed if he understands anything at all. The secret is certainly not divulged. But in the Preface we read:

> To Kant the three interests that were vital, and which lay at the centre of every thought and movement in him, were the Existence of God, the Freedom of the Will, and the Immortality of the Soul. These three positions Kant conceived himself to have demonstrated, and in the only manner at once consistent with themselves and with the thinking faculties of man. It is precisely in these themes that Hegel follows Kant. . . . Every step of his system is towards the Immortality of the Soul, every step is towards the Freedom of the Will, every step is towards God. Hegel, in truth, would restore to us all that Understanding, all that Reflexion, all that the Illumination has deprived us of, and that, too, in a higher and richer form, and not less in the light and element of the Illumination itself, and in perfect harmony with its principle and truth. (p. lxxii)

From this we see that philosophers who fail to avoid the utmost obscurity in the argumentative and demonstrative parts of their work manage to be clear enough when they come to state their conclusions. The text may be in cipher, but the title or preface is in clear. It is, of course, extremely difficult to dispose of an unintelligible argument. Of this advantage Stirling appears to be conscious. In his first chapter, on Hegel's ''Difficulty'', he says that there are many ''who actually acknowledge their inability to *construe* (though for the most part, at the same time, with the consistency of an ostrich, they comically assume to *confute*)''. As he is convinced that nobody has ever been able to construe except himself, he naturally feels himself in an impregnable position, for he says: "I have no evidence that any man has thoroughly understood Kant except Hegel, or that this latter himself remains aught else than a problem, whose solution has been arrogated, but never effected" (pp. 2, 14).

After this, in the later years of the century, among the English Idealists, Kant came to be looked on rather as the Old Testament, completed, though not exactly superseded, by Hegel's New Testament. Stirling's references to God, immortality, and free-will betray the grounds for this popularity. We want to believe that the highest authority in the universe is on our side. Our human friends and patrons are not always as powerful as we could wish; many objectionable people are more successful than they ought to be, and our own merits are not sufficiently rewarded. Yet if this is merely a temporary state of affairs, if we can feel assured that in the end the wicked will be suitably chastised and the virtuous rewarded, then we can be patient. But this prospect depends on three conditions. There must be a master of the universe whose views coincide with our own. There must be an extension of time beyond death, for it is obvious that justice is not always done in this life. Finally, we must believe that the wicked are so deliberately and that it is their own fault, for only so can we justify our resentment against them. The remaining tenets of Christianity depend to a large extent on these three essentials, and hence the trouble taken by so many philosophers to find independent support for them.

Kant himself was not insensible of the need to find an answer to scepticism and atheism. His *Kritik* did not become popular until the second edition appeared in 1787, a year after the death of Frederick the Great, under whose successor liberal publications could no longer count on royal protection. And so we find that, whereas in the first edition Kant had prefaced that "our age is the age of criticism to which everything must be subjected", including "the sacredness of religion'', in the revised Preface to the second edition he wrote that he ''must abolish knowledge in order to make room for faith''. Once again we see that the Preface is clear enough, however abstruse the text. However, religious apology was not Kant's principal aim, and many who welcomed his philosophy seem to have been more concerned with its religious usefulness than he was himself. I have noted a number of passages where he suggests how important his discoveries are, and the conviction of his own superior understanding does seem to have been one of the driving forces behind his work. His frequent references to the vain efforts of previous metaphysicians, to the impossibility of solving the main problems of philosophy without the aid of the method invented by himself, show the part played by his work in flattering his self-esteem. He has a remarkable faith in his powers of abstraction and seems to believe that he has penetrated deeply into the nature of the human mind. And the more complex his statement of this is, the more profound he supposes the whole ratiocination to be. His involved style is relevant here. We need not suppose that he deliberately wrapped up his thoughts to make them seem more profound, but this is what he has accomplished. There is a kind of subconscious dishonesty to which philosophers and literary men seem especially inclined. Since their doctrine can seldom be applied in any practical operation, and since, therefore, it can rarely be incontestably refuted, they do not need to stake their merits on truth or usefulness, but are tempted to make a show of profundity.

That many of Kant's readers were impressed by the difficulty of his text is certain. It is a fateful fact that men are easily impressed by what they do not understand and are apt to treat straightforward and clearly intelligible writing with much less respect. It is widely believed that 'profound' truths are inaccessible to common minds, and so those who do not wish their minds to be thought common are loth to admit that they do not understand.

Later commentators on Kant usually make some nominal reservations while paying homage to him. A few corrections and criticisms suggest competence and independence in the critic. Such 'expositions' of Kant's philosophy in fact explain very little, but merely repeat Kant's propositions in different order and garnish them with more of the same kind. We may, however, take heart when we find in Macaulay a writer who did not join the chorus of assent nor delude himself that he understood writing which others alleged to be profound. He noted in his diary (23 November, 1848) that he had just received a translation of Kant which he found "utterly unintelligible", and added:

> It seems to me that it ought to be possible to explain a true theory of metaphysics in words which I can understand. I can understand Locke, and Berkeley, and Hume, and Reid, and Stewart. I can understand Cicero's Academics and most of Plato: and it seems odd that in a book on the elements of metaphysics . . . I should not be able to comprehend a word.[10]

5

RECONCILING RELIGION
WITH SCIENCE

Some philosophers look askance on any alliance between religion and science, and seek rather to re-establish the prestige of the former by discrediting the latter. Wherever in the widening field of science some sign of weakness appears—when, for instance, doubt is cast on so-called basic principles, or when new phenomena emerge that will not fit current theories—there the champion of faith leaps eagerly on his prey. Others, however, try to reconcile the two. A. N. Whitehead declares in his *Process and Reality* (Cambridge: Cambridge University Press, 1929, p. 21) that "philosophy . . . attains its chief importance by fusing . . . . religion and science into one rational scheme of thought". No particular religious creed is mentioned, but the reader is free to interpret the term in a manner favourable to his own beliefs; for it seems to be generally felt that, so long as some kind of basis for a religious outlook can be established, however indeterminate, there need be no great difficulty in adjusting the details to suit one's personal requirements.

Whitehead argues that "religion should connect the rational generality of philosophy with the emotions and purposes springing out of existence in a particular society, in a particular epoch, and conditioned by particular antecedents" (p. 21). By "generality" he seems to mean generalisation. So religion connects philosophy with emotions, and (from the first passage quoted) philosophy connects religion with science.

In what follows on p. 21 I find it helpful to translate what he says into straightforward English:

Religion is an ultimate craving to infuse into the insistent particularity of emotion that non-temporal generality which primarily belongs to conceptual thought alone.

Translation: Religion seeks to make the promptings of emotion as respectable as the formulas of science. Or perhaps: religion seeks to establish the scientific validity of the beliefs prompted by our desires and fears. (This is, of course, true.)

Religion is the translation of general ideas into particular thoughts, particular emotions, and particular purposes: it is directed to the end of stretching individual interest beyond its self-defeating particularity.

Translation: Religion teaches us to behave ourselves.

In the higher organisms the differences of tempo between the mere emotions and the conceptual experiences produce a life-tedium, unless this supreme fusion [between religion and philosophy] has been effected.

Translation: The discrepancy between our dreams and the inexorable facts of life distresses us until we receive the reassurances of religion.

The two sides of the organism require a reconciliation in which emotional experiences illustrate a conceptual justification, and conceptual experiences find an emotional illustration.

Translation: It would be nice if one could enjoy the pleasures of scientific speculation without being depressed by the implications of one's conclusions.

When Whitehead adds that "religion is centred upon the harmony of rational thought with the sensitive reaction to the percepta from which experience originates", and that "science is concerned with the harmony of rational thought with the percepta themselves" (pp. 21–22), I suspect that he is merely reiterating that religion is concerned with the validity of the dream-world and science with that of the real world. He goes on:

Religion deals with the formation of the experiencing subject; whereas science deals with the objects, which are the data forming the primary phase in this experience. The subject originates from, and amid, given conditions; science conciliates thought with this primary matter of fact; and religion conciliates the thought involved in the process with the sensitive reaction involved in that same process.

We are not enlightened by being told that "the subject" (each individual person) "originates from, and amid, given conditions". Everything which has not existed from all eternity must have originated under given conditions. As for "science conciliat(ing) thought with this primary matter of fact", we do not need science to discover (or to conciliate thought with the fact) that we all originate from and amid given conditions. The task of science is to discover what these conditions are. What is the "process" which, we are here told, involves a "thought" and a "sensitive reaction"? Whitehead tells us that "the process is nothing else than the experiencing subject itself". The process, then, is only the "subject" in disguise, so that what is happening is that religion is conciliating (that is, reconciling) the thought and the "sensitive reaction" of the subject. The upshot is that there are two acts of conciliation, one performed by science, the other by religion. The things conciliated are:

1. (by science) thought and the primary matter of fact (viz. that the subject originates from, and amid, given conditions).

2. (by religion) the thought of the subject and his sensitive reaction.

We observe that in each case it is thought which has to be reconciled with something. Finally, "in this explanation [sic] it is presumed that an experiencing subject is one occasion of sensitive reaction to an actual world". So when it is asserted that a sensitive reaction is involved in an experiencing subject, the meaning is that the subject is one occasion of sensitive reaction to an actual world.

The naive view of the matter—which has much to recommend it—is that there are a number of things in the world which we knock up against from time to time, forming ideas of them as best we may and, to some extent, reflecting on them; in some cases getting to like them and in others not. Some of them are found to be helpful and desirable, others the reverse. We try and cultivate the former and avoid, or eliminate, the latter, but we do not always succeed, and have to suffer a good deal, one way and another, from the second class. Now science does mitigate, to some extent, the disagreeable features of the world, but at times and in some respects it aggravates them, and it altogether fails to preserve for us many of the things which we treasure most. On the other hand religion comforts us with the assurance that all our sufferings will find ample compensation in the end, but this fair prospect is somewhat remote. Science, so far as it goes, alleviates our present ills. We are thankful for these small mercies and would gladly have more of them. We should be sorry to forgo the benefits of science even if we are not among those for whom it is a means of livelihood and a source of honour. But the success of science in dealing with the things and events in the world is based on the patient study of these things and events, which often reveals unexpected and unwelcome relations between them, conflicting with certain religious beliefs. We desire the benefits of science but we do not want to forgo the promises of religion. We are therefore grateful to our philosophers who reassure us, and especially to those who seem to speak with the authority of science and declare that all its revelations are in perfect harmony with our religious aspirations. The gist of Whitehead's message seems to be that such reassurance is needed by many who feel their religion to have lately grown a little insecure.

Whitehead calls "the final real things" of which, in his view, the world is made up "actual entities" (p. 24), and says:

> . . . the reasons for things are always to be found in the composite nature of definite actual entities—in the nature of God for reasons of the highest absoluteness, and in the nature of definite temporal actual entities for reasons which refer to a particular environment. The ontological principle can be summarized as: no actual entity, then no reason. (p. 25)

The "ontological principle", then, amounts to this: if you cannot find an "actual entity", you can explain nothing. One such entity is God, and so the reasons for something may be in God. He adds:

> Each actual entity is analysable in an indefinite number of ways . . . . The analysis of an actual entity into 'prehensions' is that mode of analysis which exhibits the most concrete elements in the nature of actual entities.

A "prehension" is what the rest of us call a thought or an idea.

A prehension reproduces in itself the general characteristics of an actual entity; it is referent to an external world, and in this sense will be
said to have a 'vector character'; it involves emotion, and purpose,
and valuation, and causation. In fact, any characteristic of an actual
entity is reproduced in a prehension. It might have been a complete
actuality; but by reason of a certain incomplete partiality, a prehension is only a subordinate element in an actual entity. A reference to
the complete actuality is required to give the reason why such a
prehension is what it is in respect to its subjective form. This subjective form is determined by the subjective aim at further integration,
so as to obtain the 'satisfaction' of the completed subject. In other
words, final causation and atomism are interconnected philosophical
principles. (pp. 25–26)

Shall we venture on an interpretation in simple language? The
"subjective form" is the idea which a man forms of an object, and the "subjective aim", his purpose, if he has any, in
regard to it. His "aim at further integration" will then
perhaps be his desire to explain, interpret, and generalise
phenomena. The prehension is a man's conception of an object, which is coloured by emotion, purpose, etc. I do not
know quite how to fit in causation. Is it the man's notion of
the cause of the object, or the cause of the man's notion?
Possibly both. What is the "vector character" of a prehension? It is the orientation of a man towards an object, his approval, disapproval, desire for, fear of, indifference to, an
object. Different individuals have different prehensions of
the same actual entity, hence the analysis of the latter. The
reproduction in the prehension of the general characteristics
of an actual entity is the resemblance between the idea which
the man forms and the object of which he forms it. If this interpretation is correct we may translate the paragraph into
English as follows: Every object may be conceived in a
number of ways, and each manner of conceiving it leads to a
different set of ideas. These ideas represent the characters of
the thing, but they are coloured with emotions, fears, and
desires, which define the attitude of the man to the thing. The
idea is never a perfect representation of the thing, but, such
as it is, it is derived from the thing and can be explained only
by reference to things in general. The imperfect correspondence between ideas and reality is due to human frail-
ty. This is no more than the vulgar, naive account of the matter, but I must confess to the suspicion that, in spite of the

pretentious language, Whitehead means nothing more abstruse than this.

We cannot dispose of this kind of 'philosophy' by disputing about it. The multitude of meaningless words, or words with indeterminate meanings, yields for every page of such a book a number of conceivable interpretations beyond the reach of the most industrious criticism. One can only protest that abstract ideas cannot be represented by definitions. They must be laboriously built up, sometimes over years. If a man reaches a new abstraction from a new selection of concretes, he must expect, if he wishes to be understood, to have to illustrate it extensively and rehearse the process by which he attained it. Terms used to represent abstract ideas may be bandied about by anybody, but if the speaker has not himself formed the abstraction the sequence of words uttered will have no more meaning than the creaking of a gate.

The abstractions of mathematics and of the physical sciences are built up gradually and in an orderly sequence from very simple and familiar concrete notions, which are numerous and readily presented. Not only are the elementary concretes accessible, but the highest abstractions are attained gradually by way of abstractions of more limited range. The educational sequence has been elaborated over many generations and is based on the original sequence in which the successive abstractions were first attained (cf. above, p. 52). In short all the conditions are favourable for the gradual formation of these abstract ideas and, not least important, there is a general uniformity of terminology. Everything is thus made as easy as possible for the student who would arrive at the abstract ideas required in mathematics and the physical sciences. Even so, it still requires several years of special study to acquire the ability to make use of them. It would not take long to learn to pronounce the words, and employ them in perfectly grammatical sentences, but the better part of a lifetime is barely sufficient to enable a man to make consistent and intelligible use of the terms which represent the highest current abstractions of mathematics and physics.

If the generalisations of philosophy are wider than those of mathematics and physics, it may be supposed that few will attain to them, and those few only after the labours of a life-time. But unfortunately they do not at present constitute an established and generally accepted system with an agreed terminology. Many attempts have been made independently, and the successive stages by which the most abstract ideas have been reached have not been always the same, so that the results are not comparable. Unless the philosopher retraces for us the successive steps by which he attained his highest generalisation, amply illustrated at each stage, it will be impossible for us to understand any single statement he may make about his final results.

Whitehead succeeds in making one thing plain in an otherwise incomprehensible book, namely that religion has nothing to fear from the conclusions at which his metaphysic arrives. As a vindication of religious prepossessions a book is none the less effectual for being obscure. The faithful do not need to follow the argument, and the sceptics cannot.

6

THE NEW THEOLOGY

In *The Observer* on 17 March 1963 appeared an article by the then Bishop of Woolwich, Dr. J. A. T. Robinson, entitled 'Our image of God must go', introducing his new book *Honest to God*, which thereafter proved immensely successful. In the article he showed himself willing to sacrifice belief in God as a supernatural person and in the "religious frame" within which the Christian faith is offered to the believer. In return for these concessions he hoped to be allowed to retain the beliefs that 1. "God is ultimate reality (that's what we mean by the word)"; 2. "mathematics is God"; 3. "what we see in Jesus of Nazareth is a window through the surface of things into the very ground of our being"; 4. "depth is what the word God means".

Now it really does not seem from this that Robinson was offering to give up very much that the ordinary Christian would miss. And it is hard to see why there should be required what he called "radical reformulations for the Church in almost every field—of doctrine, worship, ethics and evangelism", for if words may be given new meanings to suit modern requirements, there is no reason why the words themselves should be altered. When the Christian *says*: 'I believe in God the Father, God the Son, and God the Holy Ghost', he will mean: 'I believe in Ultimate Reality, in Mathematics, and in Depth'. But he will not need to 'reformulate' what he says.

Apropos of the "radical reformulations" Robinson said: "This is a dangerous process, but immensely exhilarating; and the exciting thing is that it is not being forced upon the Church from outside but is welling up from within". Certainly nobody outside the Church is in a position to "force" new ideas upon it. On the other hand, nobody outside the Church has any reason to complain if it at long last begins to discard some of the primitive notions discarded long ago by deistic or atheistic philosophers. As long as it seemed at all possible, the Church exerted its authority to discourage and even to persecute every kind of 'heresy'. When the heretics look like outnumbering the orthodox, the time has come for a 'refor- mulation', and Robinson was thrilled by the thought that this is a spontaneous movement from within the Church.

But, as he said, "this is a dangerous process". It *is* dan- gerous, for two chief reasons. The more naive, and per- haps more sincere, followers of Christ may be disturbed when they learn that so much of what they have always be- lieved and been taught is now declared by their respected teachers to be little better than moonshine. And the more sceptical brethren may be tempted to carry their critical ques- tionings even further than the Bishop.

In *Honest to God* Robinson followed a technique com- mon among recent Christian apologists, particularly among those on whom he relied (Bultmann, Tillich, Bonhoeffer). These apologists do not find it possible to defend traditional Christian beliefs, such as Jesus's virgin birth, his miracles, and his resurrection, but they nonetheless wish to suggest that abandoning all this leaves the Christian with the same God he has always worshipped and the same Jesus in whom he has always trusted. To achieve this end, they use language whose terms are so vague and uncertain in meaning that anyone can subscribe to their propositions without the feeling that he is saying what he does not believe. The terms are nevertheless familiar ones. It is inevitable that very many common words should have a number of meanings, and in normal inter- course the meaning of such words is explained by the context or by the situation in which they are used. In a context which consists almost entirely of equally ambiguous words there is no possibility of determining the meaning; yet the familiarity of the separate words makes the unwary reader suppose that there must be some meaning behind the whole proposition.

A good example is Robinson's discussion of the idea of

God. He wished to get rid of the ideas which have hitherto been associated with the Christian belief in God and substitute a new idea, but still to be able to use the word 'God'; and his new idea was that "the word 'God' denotes the ultimate depth of all our being, the creative ground and meaning of all our existence".[1] But do these words really convey any intelligible ideas? How can 'being' be said to have 'depth'? These must be metaphors. And what is to be understood by "all our being"? Is it the being of all of us, or all the being of each one of us? And can we conceive less than all the being of anything that is? The being of something must be what it is. Part of the being of anything may mean what it partly is, or part of what it is. The verb 'to be' is a very useful auxiliary, but as a substantive verb it derives its meaning from the context, and the context here does not help us. Is there any difference between 'being' and 'existence'? And what is the ground of existence? What, in particular, is the creative ground? The book is filled with these phrases, and the plausibility of all the arguments it contains depends on the very dubious assumption that they do mean something.

Robinson discussed Psalm 139 from the standpoint of his new theology. He did not dispute the Psalmist's statements that our downsitting and uprising are known and our thought understood afar off; that there is not a word in our tongue, but lo, it is known altogether, and we are beset behind and before. But, following Tillich, he maintained that it is not God as usually understood who knows and understands and besets us, but "the ground of our being" (pp. 57–59). So the Psalmist was quite right and we may go on singing, reciting or quoting the familiar words without compunction, merely substituting for 'God' under our breath 'the ground of our being'. It is very important that we should not be forced to give up all the best-known passages in the Bible, because they reveal primitive notions about God and Justice. So we must reinterpret them. This is, of course, no new practice. It has been the principal task of the commentator at all times to reconcile the inspired word of God with the reason and conscience of man.

Then Robinson breaks into a new definition, saying that

what is of "ultimate significance" in the constitution of the universe is love, and therefore that the real meaning of the word 'God' is love. He says:

> To believe in God as love means to believe that in pure personal relationship we encounter, not merely what ought to be, but what is, the deepest, veriest truth about the structure of reality. This, in face of all the evidence, is a tremendous act of faith. But it is not the feat of persuading oneself of the existence of a super-Being beyond this world endowed with personal qualities. Belief in God is the trust, the wellnigh incredible trust, that to give ourselves to the uttermost in love is not to be confounded but to be 'accepted', that Love is the ground of our being, to which ultimately we 'come home'. (p. 49)

What is meant by "pure personal relationship"? How many degrees of depth and "veriness" has truth? What is the "structure of reality"? What is involved or implied in being "accepted"? By whom or what is one accepted? Do we "come home" to our being, to the ground of our being, or to love? And why home? Have we been there before? With so many ambiguities and uncertainties in this short passage, it is obvious that the meaning is indeterminate.

We also read that "our experience of God is distinctively and characteristically an awareness of the transcendent, the numinous, the unconditional" (p. 52). Perhaps if we knew what was meant by the "numinous" and by the "unconditional" we should be in a better position to interpret the "transcendent". Unfortunately these things are equally mysterious. Of course we know the meaning of 'unconditional surrender' and similar phrases, where the adjective merely stands for 'without limiting conditions'. But when the adjective is used without any noun expressed or implied it means nothing. The mere absence of anything is nothing. How, for example, could we conceive an absence of lobsters? We could only think of some other things which were not absent but were commonly associated with lobsters, as pots or mayonnaise. But an absence of conditions is the more difficult to conceive even in this indirect fashion since the word 'condition' has many more meanings than 'lobster'. We speak of the conditions which determine an event, of the condition of an invalid, of a car, of a country, of the conditions of an agreement, of a conditioned reflex. What sort of a conception can we frame out of nothing but the absence of any kind of conditions? Abstractions of this kind, because they lack any intelligible meaning, can be used to make propositions which cannot possibly be refuted, and to suggest profound significance which escapes the reach of meaner minds.

The year 1963 saw the publication not only of *Honest to God* but also of four essays by Cambridge theologians to form a volume entitled *Objections to Christian Belief*. Its aim was to answer *supposed* objections, and it was not an attack but a defence. Some of the defence consists in the technique already illustrated from *Honest to God*. Here, for instance, is how J. S. Bezzant argued for a personal God:

> As personality is the highest category we know which the world-ground has produced, the possibility of which must have been present in the primary collocations of the universe, whatever they were, there is good ground for ascribing personality to its originator, provided we remember not to over-personalize the world-ground, or God.[2]

What is personality? Has a spider or a mushroom personality, or is it something peculiar to man? If so how can it be recognised? Is it present in idiots? Is it in any way related to the body and in particular to the brain? And what do we understand by the "primary collocations of the universe"? Does this mean the primeval chaos when darkness was upon the face of the deep, or is it the original universe as it issued from the hands of the maker before the processes of evolution had got under way? And why must personality or the possibility of personality have been present at that time? Could the creator not have added it later? Or, having set his universe going, did he cease to interfere with it? And what is meant by over-personalising the world-ground? Does it mean attributing an excess of personality to God? Bezzant added: "No one has or can have exhaustive knowledge of God as he is in himself. Human personality may be, indeed must be, but a faint copy of Divine personality." Does this mean that there must be a great deal more personality in God than there is in man? Yet we are to beware of over-personalising the world-ground. What is a "copy" of the personality of God, and how can it be faint or otherwise? And what would be the reverse of faint in this connection?

In his review of *Objections to Christian Belief* in *The Observer* on 14 April 1963, Philip Toynbee stated that Dr. Bezzant's essay used "the weapons of modern linguistic philosophy with terrible effect", and that the other contributors to the volume had likewise made telling points against traditional Christian beliefs; one had "castigated the harsh and trivial legalism of the Church", while another had admitted that "there are many and powerful psychological objections to the Church's current attitudes" and had attacked "the hypocrisy of those Christians who are totally unaware of their own motives". Toynbee then added that "the obvious next step . . . would be for a group of intellectual non-believers to write with equal harshness about the contradictions or inadequacies of their own beliefs". But so far as the unbelief of the non-believers refers simply to Christianity and religion, why should there be contradictions and inadequacies in their beliefs? Furthermore, the four authors of *Objections to Christian Belief* were not, presumably, criticising their *own* beliefs. They did not, I take it, themselves stand by the "harsh and trivial legalism of the Church", nor maintain those "attitudes" to which there are so many powerful psychological objections; nor were they so hypocritical as to be unaware of their own motives, nor so obstinate as to cling to beliefs which have been demolished by the terrible weapons of modern linguistic philosophy.

Perhaps Toynbee would have been glad to have some arguments in favour of religion. Since the theologians seem more successful in attacking than in defending it, he turned to the unbelievers and asked them to supply a few arguments on the other side. He said in effect: We cannot forgo religion, but we can find no good reason for preserving it. Our religious leaders are not helpful. You who have spent your lives attacking it must know better than anyone the weaknesses in your own arguments. Let us hear from you. The theologians have been generous in granting most of your points. Can you not meet them half-way?

Toynbee went on to express sympathy with "the Christian conviction that there exists a reality other than and better than the reality witnessed by the senses", and complained that "the more intolerant rationalists . . . reject all mystical experience". The following week *The Observer* published a letter from Juliet Rhys Williams, which stated: "As Philip Toynbee points out . . . rationalists have most irrationally refused to include within their philosophy a large field of human experience, including mystical and aesthetic experience and 'the pressing claims of parapsychology'." What she must mean is that rationalists have explained these things the wrong way, for they have certainly not ignored them. The mystics explain mysticism as the manifestation of something supernatural or divine. Those who are not mystics offer other explanations. Ms. Rhys Williams did not distinguish between experiences and the interpretation of experiences. Unfortunately our psychologists are not very successful in explaining any part of human behaviour, so that it is hardly surprising that they should have failed to deal adequately with these rather exceptional forms of experience.

Time like an ever-rolling stream bears Robinson, Toynbee, and the rest away. What remains from century to century is the tendency towards hocus-pocus which is manifest in these authors. By this term I understand that form of writing or speaking which presumes on the credulity, simplicity, or benevolence of the hearer. One cannot always distinguish between deliberate fraud and unintentional verbiage. The practice of writing is so common, and the facility for constructing conventional sentences so independent of any ability to conduct one's thoughts in an orderly and consistent manner, that our contemporary literature is very largely composed of verbal reflexes, forms of speech which have been learned through being constantly heard and read, which become vaguely associated with certain general emotional situations but are not linked to any clear idea. Verbal reflexes are, of course, necessary in speech. Rapid communication is dependent on them, but their use can be exaggerated, and then we get verbiage. Much of this is not at all deliberate and arises in part from the desire to write well. Unfortunately there are different standards of good writing. So long as this is understood to mean simply clear and intelligible writing and nothing else, then the practice will not lead to verbiage or hocus-pocus. But if good writing is supposed to mean arranging words in certain effective patterns, then it is obvious that the relation between one word and the next will seem more important than the relation between the words and their meaning. But the desire to write well is only one of the motives which tend to corrupt language. Among certain writers we find the desire to impress the reader not so much by felicity of expression as with the writer's depth of thought. Profound thought is usually supposed to involve abstruse expression, and the indulgent or modest reader may readily mistake obscurity for depth. There are, no doubt, writers who are willing to exploit such simplicity, but for one such deliberate mountebank there are perhaps hundreds of honest folk who mistake their own mental confusion for inspiration. Being unacquainted with the reality of abstract thought they mistake the mist for a mountain. Since abstract ideas are very difficult to manipulate in one's reflections, one tends to substitute symbols (cf. below, p. 80). With due precautions this is permissible, but when the symbol is merely a word there is little beside speech reflexes and literary conventions and traditional jargon to ensure consistency and significance in its use.

PART THREE

VERBIAGE
AND PHILOSOPHY

7

THINGS, IDEAS, AND WORDS

Those who have tried to learn or teach a language without resort to any form of translation know that the process necessarily involves continual reference to the concrete world. It is thus that the child learns to speak his own language, and thus the traveller learns to speak the language of the aboriginal. Thus too must every scientist or philosopher, introducing new terms, explain their meaning by relating them to some perceptible reality, some experimental event, some repeatable structure of things or sequence of occurrences. All the pompous paraphernalia of description and verbal definition, unless it rests ultimately upon a basis of recoverable concrete experience, can convey nothing. Since experiences can be recalled by association, when conventional signs or sounds have become associated with particular experiences, the latter can be recalled by the former. This is the secret of linguistic communication. But if the sign or the sound has not been associated with the same experience by the persons using it, it cannot serve the purpose of communication.

It is things, situations, and processes with which we have to deal and which science investigates. Our thoughts or ideas about them are the result of our study and observations, and consist partly of memory and partly of imagination. According as these thoughts are more or less adequate to the things from which they are derived, so our dealings with the things themselves will be more or less successful—indeed we can only judge their adequacy from the success which attends our application of them. The words which we attach to the things, or to our ideas, are little more than labels and, apart from this connection, are no more significant than the ticket which the cloakroom attendant attaches to our umbrella. When we present our ticket he knows what it means because he has taken the trouble to associate it (by means of a duplicate) with the article it represents; and our hearer knows what our words mean when we speak to him, because he has learned to associate the words with the same things as ourselves. If he has not, then we cannot communicate with him by means of words.

Thus language may be a very efficient means of communication when there is adequate previous understanding between the communicating parties. But where there is no such collusion, where the parties are strangers with only a minimum of common experience, even the smallest piece of specific information may be very difficult to impart. Indeed, so hard is it to express briefly in words the idea of even a simple concrete object which cannot be represented as a mere combination of things already familiar, that in serious treatises diagrams, drawings, photographs, or mathematical symbols are invariably relied upon to supplement verbal descriptions. But apart from technicalities we do not often have to suggest wholly new ideas to one another; most of our ideas are derived from things known equally well to all our hearers, and if we have, from personal experience, special knowledge about a thing, such knowledge is often irrelevant for all practical purposes. If a man inquires how he may get to Paddington, I may advise him to take a 27 bus, and this concise piece of information will suffice to get him there. To me the 27 bus may stand for a very complicated idea, including the names and nature of all the buildings on the route, the width of the streets, the character of the illumination, the number of fire hydrants and pillar-boxes, the average frequency of patrolling policemen, but all this is irrelevant, and the fact that the formula does not convey any of this makes it rather more than less useful.

The concrete world is inexhaustible in its complexity, and it is obvious that all the languages of men added together could not furnish words enough to match a single aspect of it. If description required any degree of correspondence between the array of noises that constitute language and the array of things which constitute the universe, then no description would be possible. But description requires nothing of the kind. The word 'street' may at once evoke a fully adequate representation of a scene whose real details could never be enumerated. The reality is already immensely simplified in the memory and imagination, but the idea is linguistically represented by a mere hissing through the teeth. The noise which constitutes the word needs no greater complexity than suffices to distinguish it from other words with which it might be confounded. Three letters are enough to represent a bee, yet volumes would be needed to contain all that is known about the animal.

Complaints about the defects and inadequacies of language became common after the Renaissance, when all kinds of things were discovered and investigated which had no names, so that thinking with non-verbal imagery became unavoidable. Of course, ordinary people had always thought in that way, as they still do; but it was only the philosophers who discussed the nature of thinking, and they had only their own experience to work on. Bacon called words the Idols of the Marketplace; and Descartes clearly recognised that thinking involves something else besides words, but complained that it is all too easy to substitute words for ideas. This, he said, is why people

> often assent to propositions which they do not understand, and which they do not even try to understand, either because they believe that they once understood them, or because they suppose their teachers understood them, and they must have imbibed the meaning with the words.[1]

Descartes figures in the histories of philosophy chiefly on account of his metaphysical speculations, but his physiological theories were based on his own practical investigations; and to fit a theory of nervous action into the anatomical intricacies displayed by dissection to the eyes and fingers requires the mental manipulation of visual and tactile ideas and not merely words. Hallam, whose ideas on the subject may have been derived chiefly from books, speaks disparagingly of Descartes's physiology[2] but Sherrington, who understood the problem a little more clearly, was better able to appreciate Descartes's views.[3]

In 1684 Leibniz observed that in our thoughts we often substitute signs for things. When, for instance,

> I think of a chiliogon, or polygon with a thousand equal sides, I do not always consider the nature of a side, of equality, and of the number thousand (or of the cube of ten); but these words, the sense of which presents itself to my mind in an obscure, or at least imperfect manner, take the place to me of the ideas which I have of them, because my memory attests to me that I know the signification of these words, and that their explanation is not now necessary for any judgment.[4]

He calls this "blind" or "symbolical" thought, in distinction from "intuitive" thought, which is thought which consists in the imagined appearance of a thing, its sound, shape, or smell, and he goes on to speak of the dangers attending "symbolical" thought, in language which reminds us of the words of Descartes already quoted.

Hume, without referring to Leibniz, discusses this same phenomenon in a manner which implies that in his view it is not intuitive but only symbolical thinking that stands in need of explanation. He says:

> I believe every one who examines the situation of his mind in reasoning, will agree with me, that we do not annex distinct and complete ideas to every term we make use of; and that in talking of *government, church, negotiation, conquest*, we seldom spread out in our minds all the simple ideas of which these complex ones are composed. It is however observable, that notwithstanding this imperfection, we may avoid talking nonsense on these subjects, and may perceive any repugnance among the ideas as well as if we had a full comprehension of them. Thus if, instead of saying, that, *in war, the weaker have always recourse to negotiations*, we should say, that *they have always recourse to conquest*, the custom which we have acquired, of attributing certain relations to ideas, still follows the words, and makes us immediately perceive the absurdity of that proposition.[5]

Words serve a real and important purpose in the reflective process, as a mnemonic.[6] They become associated with things, but also with one another, not chiefly through their sound but in the muscular movements by which we utter them. We are able to learn to pronounce long sequences of words, thousands at a time. They need not be visualised, but are committed to the muscular memory and can be repeated in the correct sequence as often as we like. I do not know whether some people are able to hear long speeches in their auditory imagination without taking any muscular part in their delivery, but I think such persons must be exceptional. At any rate there is no doubt that most people have a considerable memory for the utterance of verbal sequences and some possess the capacity in an extraordinary degree.

Now since words acquire an independent association with ideas and things, this recording in the memory of word sequences has a valuable mnemonic function. Ideas are also linked together in the memory and one idea recalls another. But ideas have multiple associations and are always highly composite. To establish a one-dimensional chain of ideas in the memory would mean annulling all lateral linkages, and each component idea would have to be reduced to some brief and restricted representative element. In fact, when we allow our memory to be freely active the course of associated recollections is never the same, and this apparently random ebb and flow of thoughts is the source of all novelty and invention. But when experiment has taught us how to achieve our end we need to remember how the thing was done. It may be that a long succession of related acts was involved, performed in definite order. If the sequence of acts can be repeated until it is acquired as a habit, then there will be no further need for reflection. Such a complex piece of behaviour is likely to depend in detail on the momentary circumstances. We learn to play a sonata and always repeat each movement in exactly the same way, but we could not learn in the same manner to play an innings at cricket or to dismantle a complicated piece of machinery. No verbal formula will help us in the case of cricket, but where the action in question consists of a large number of component acts each one of which presents no difficulty, then all that must be committed to memory is the order in which they are to be carried out. If each act can be represented by a word or phrase, then all that is necessary is to commit to memory the succession of words.

This is the key to the function of language in thought. Experience has taught us to combine certain acts or to expect certain sequences or combinations of events. If these combinations or sequences are not too extensive we may remember them in a more direct way, but where they involve too many components we find it easier to represent the latter by words, and link the words in our memory. The verbal formulas thus recorded can be recalled when required by merely initiating the sequence of words. We recall the first phrase of the formula and the rest is revived automatically. With its aid the whole complex of acts or events or circumstances is reconstructed in the imagination. These remembered word sequences are merely a machinery for the more systematic organisation of memory. They represent the things with which they are associated only in the sense that they are able to revive the thoughts of them in the memory. We cannot experiment with the words as we can experiment with visual, tactile, or auditory images. If the latter are but an imperfect substitute for the real objects, the words are an even more imperfect substitute for the visual, auditory, and tactile ideas. In a great many simple and concrete cases reasoning may be carried on for a short time by verbal formula. Particular cases are expressed in words and then referred to a general precept or rule. Where the facts are familiar and the correlations well-known, we may get to use the verbal expression in our thoughts without any recall of tangible experiences. From the bare statement in the news bulletin that it is going to rain we may decide on a course of action that is appropriate without any imaginative representation of streaming windows or soaked ground. From the verbal announcement of a particular event we may jump directly to the verbal statement of the probable consequence without the mediation of any concrete imagery. But this can happen only if the linkage is familiar and habitual. There is no safeguard against false inference in the nature of the words themselves. The words are only arbitrarily associated with the ideas and the latter may only imperfectly represent the real things. It is therefore only in the realm of customary events and well established correlations among familiar things that inferences from verbal formulas, unsupported by any reference, either external or imaginative, are not precarious.

Unfortunately there are certain regions of thought where the most abstract ideas are the principal topic and where in consequence there is no simple imaginative substitute for words. The concrete foundation of a highly abstract idea is apt to be so vast that there is no room for it in the mind of the philosopher, whatever species of symbolic representation he may employ. But just where the idea expands beyond the capacity of the speculative mind

> Da stellt ein Wort zur rechten Zeit sich ein.[7]

A train of thought involves reminiscence and organisation of memories. Different individuals, apart from differences in experience, have different capacities for both of these. They may use the same words to designate their ideas, but there may nevertheless be only a minimal overlap between the ideas. An engineer, a train-driver, and a schoolboy railway enthusiast may all speak of 'locomotives', but their respective ideas will differ considerably, although with sufficient in common to avoid misunderstanding when they communicate with each other. It is therefore inappropriate to speak of *the* idea of a locomotive, or of anything else. The point is well put by John Stuart Mill:

> The purposes of general names would not be answered, unless the complex idea connected with a general name in one person's mind were composed of essentially the same elements as the idea connected with it in the mind of another. There hence arises a natural illusion, making us feel as if, instead of ideas as numerous as minds, and merely resembling one another, there were one idea, independent of individual minds, and to which it is the business of each to learn to make his private idea correspond. This is the Platonic doctrine of Ideas in all its purity: and as half the speculative world are Platonists without knowing it, hence it also is that in the writings of so many psychologists we read of *the* conception or *the* concept of so and so; as if there was a concept of a thing or of a class of things, other than the ideas in individual minds—a concept belonging to everybody, the common inheritance of the human race, but independent of any of the particular minds which conceive it. In reality, however, this common concept is but the sum of the elements which it is requisite for the purposes of discourse that people should agree with one another in including in the complex idea which they associate with a class name. . . . These are only a part, and often but a small part, of each

person's complex idea, but they are the part which it is necessary should be the same in all.[8]

The term *concept* is currently used as a synonym for *idea*. Concepts are referred to as if they had an objective existence as concrete as a cabbage. In mathematics there are ideas which are so nearly the same in the minds of mathematicians that no great error results from treating them as if they were as constant as any part of the anatomy. But in most other matters such uniformity of conception is impossible, and it is therefore misleading to speak of such 'concepts' by name as if there existed any means of discovering what the name stood for.

The real difficulty begins where there is generalisation or abstraction. So long as there exists an object which can be produced or pointed out to clinch description, there may be almost perfect congruence of thought sequences in different minds. But an abstract idea cannot be replaced in any phase of communication by a presentable concrete. The idea of an insect, for instance, includes—at any rate in the mind of the entomologist—that of a beetle, a fly, a grasshopper, a bee, a bug, and so on. His idea of a beetle will already be highly general, for it is likely to include that of a Carabid, a Scarab, a Weevil, etc. Common to all beetles are certain characters, and it is in virtue of these that the various species which possess them are classified as beetles. It is possible to think of these common characters by themselves, forgetting for the moment all the other properties which belong to the separate species; and by this process of subtraction we form in our minds what may be called the *abstract* beetle—a kind of scarecrow, a flimsy skeleton of a creature which has very little resemblance to any real beetle. By taking a smaller group, say the Carabids or the Weevils, we can form a less airy abstraction. The number of common characters will be greater and will come nearer to constituting a possible animal. Thus the larger the number of individuals from which we make our abstraction, the smaller will be the set of characters that constitutes the abstraction.

It is, however, sometimes supposed that the act of

abstraction applies to what is discarded rather than to what is retained: all the properties except the one (or several) we are concerned with are, on this view, said to have been abstracted. We 'abstract from them' or 'make abstraction from them', in the sense that we ignore them. This is dangerous, for it allows what remains after they have been thought away to be left unmentioned. Kant, for instance, 'abstracts' whatever he wants to get rid of and is then free to assume that there is always something left, however much is 'abstracted'. He thinks he may abstract *from* anything he likes to mention, without looking for any evidence that the process leaves a remainder. He seems to take for granted that something *must* be left even if it is quite impossible to conceive it.[9] And this difficulty of conceiving the retained quality is easily overcome by the use of a word. A name can always be given, and then the word is discussed as if it stood for a real quality. As an idea becomes more and more abstract and therefore more and more empty, as it were, there is a tendency to fill it out with a kind of illegitimate upholstery. The genuine abstraction, which consists exclusively of characters common to all the individuals from which it has been drawn, is apt to be replaced by a dummy, a more concrete idea, perhaps one single individual from which the abstraction is drawn, as when the idea of a beetle in the abstract is replaced by the idea of a ladybird, and the thought-experiments which should by rights be made with the abstract beetle are made in fact with the surrogate. In this way erroneous results are likely to be obtained.

The tendency to utilise a dummy instead of a legitimate abstraction is encouraged by the use of language. Ideas get associated with words and phrases, and verbal habits are formed which tend to interfere with the normal course of thinking. The word which first symbolised a common character, when the latter is vague and difficult to imagine, comes to take its place. Furthermore, a word which is used in different contexts with different meanings is like the word which represents the abstract idea. For the latter is used for all the concretes from which the abstract idea is derived. But

in the case of the real abstraction there is something in common between all the different meanings, whereas in the case
of words which have come to be used in different contexts for
ideas having nothing in common, there is no common basis,
however abstract. Such words are, however, used like the
others, and a common character is sometimes assumed in all
the different things one such word stands for. When someone
has got into the way of thinking with terms which have never
been founded on any true process of abstraction, his propositions are uninterpretable. The naive belief that certain
abstract nouns have a constant meaning, independent of the
context in which they are used, has resulted in vast amounts
of worthless 'philosophical' writing. The next two chapters illustrate this point with reference to two twentieth-century
'philosophers'.

8

'CATEGORY MISTAKES'

Ryle's *The Concept of Mind* (London: Hutchinson, 1949) shows just how much can be accomplished by misconceptions about language. He is concerned to dispose of the view that mind and body are separate entities, that the mind is a "ghost in the machine". This, he says, is one of the many errors that can be rectified by attention to the "habits of language". The rectification consists in correcting what he calls "category mistakes". The dogma of the ghost in the machine "represents the facts of mental life as if they belonged to one logical type or category (or range of types or categories), when they actually belong to another" (p. 16).

To clarify what he means by category mistake, Ryle gives a number of examples. It is a category mistake to suppose that the University of Oxford is something separate from and additional to its colleges, museums, and offices. It is another to suppose that an army division is something separate from and additional to the battalions, brigades, etc. which compose it, and yet another to suppose that the "team-spirit" is "another cricketing-operation supplementary to all of the other special tasks". Such mistakes have been made by "people who did not know how to wield the concepts '*university*', '*division*', and '*team-spirit*'. Their puzzles arose from inability to use certain items in the English vocabulary" (p. 17). The offenders in question were, in two of the three cases, foreigners, and in the other a child. The argument seems to imply that children and foreigners may well be unable to "wield" the relevant concepts. Can it be that 'wielding a concept' merely means understanding a word? Ryle's second phrase—"inability to use certain items in the English vocabulary" would seem to suggest this. Furthermore it really is not plain what he wishes us to understand by category in this connection, for 'team-spirit' does not belong to the same category, in the usual sense of the word, as either university or division, in that team-spirit certainly is something additional to the operations of batting, bowling, fielding, and other "special tasks". All these separate operations may be executed with exemplary skill by the individual players and yet the team-spirit be lacking.

Cricket, universities, and military formations are so diverse that it is scarcely to be expected that we should be able to extract anything useful from their comparison. Every composite is something more than its parts for it includes the arrangement of these. If regarding the mind as a ghost in a bodily machine is a category mistake, and if category mistakes are made by people imperfectly acquainted with the language they are using, then why has this particular category mistake been made by so many respectable philosophers? Was Descartes merely ignorant of the French language?

When Ryle suggests that it is only a question of knowing the language, I suspect that he does not mean what most people would mean. For him, 'knowing the language' is a technical expression signifying what most people call 'knowing what one is talking about'. It has become fashionable in certain philosophical circles to treat all philosophical and scientific differences of view as differences of language. Bertrand Russell, for instance, has said that "Einstein's substitution of space-time for space and time represents a *change of language* for which there are the same sort of grounds of simplicity as there were for the Copernican *change of language*." Other of Einstein's views, he adds, "remain speculative" so that "no one would be surprised if evidence were found which would lead astronomers to give up *this way of speaking*".[1] (my italics) This passage well illustrates the prevalence of the notion that what most people call 'thinking' is in fact only talking, either audibly or in the form of muttered soliloquy.

As a further example of "the absurdity of conjoining terms of different types" Ryle mentions "the well-known joke: 'She came home in a flood of tears and a sedan-chair' "

(p. 22). There is nothing absurd in this, and the quaintness is due to the convention which prevents us from using a single preposition before two nouns when its meaning changes. It is usual in such a case to repeat the preposition. Thus we could say that she came home in a sedan chair and in a flood of tears. A man may be said to be in bed and in pain, but it sounds a little incongruous to say that he is in bed and pain. But this is a mere convention of language and has no logical significance. Ryle adds that it will also follow from his argument that

> both Idealism and Materialism are answers to an improper question. The 'reduction' of the material world to mental states and processes, as well as the 'reduction' of mental states and processes to physical states and processes, presuppose the legitimacy of the disjunction 'Either there exist minds or there exist bodies (but not both)'. It would be like saying: 'Either she bought a left-hand glove and a right-hand glove or she bought a pair of gloves (but not both)'.

In fact the "legitimacy" or otherwise of either of these propositions depends on their meaning. For the second it is easy to supply an intelligible meaning, since two gloves, even if they are respectively right and left, are not necessarily a pair, and the plausibility of the statement depends only on the probability of odd gloves being sold. But if, with Ryle, we assume the alternatives in each of the two propositions to be identical in meaning, then we must assume that he holds minds and bodies to be the same. But he will harp on his "category-mistakes", saying:

> It is perfectly proper to say, in one logical tone of voice, that there exist minds and to say, in another logical tone of voice, that there exist bodies. But these expressions . . . indicate two different senses of 'exist' . . . [It would be] . . . a poor joke . . . to say that there exist prime numbers and Wednesdays and public opinions and navies; or that there exist both minds and bodies. (p. 23)

He seems to find it ridiculous to contract four statements into one by using a single verb ('exist') in four different senses with four subjects (prime numbers, Wednesdays, etc.). The real objection to such elliptical statements is that they may be ambiguous. If I have occasion to say that a man is a liar and that he has a denture, I may express it neatly by saying that his statements and his teeth are false, and there seems little danger of my being misunderstood. But if it were necessary to explain that a man under the provocation of a curtain lecture had resorted to fiction, it might be misleading to say that all the time both parties had been lying in bed. Ryle seems to be suggesting that the statement 'bodies and minds exist' is nugatory because of the double meaning of 'exist'. Is it not then equally objectionable to say that ants and elephants exist, for the existence of an ant is very different from that of an elephant?

That much confusion results from the ambiguity of words is not to be denied; and it often arises from the assumption that some kind of reliance may be placed upon the conventions of language. The meaning of a word depends primarily on its context, and apart from some intelligible context the statement that something exists is futile. Consider the prime numbers. Prime number is a word signifying a number that has no whole factors except itself and 1. Are there such numbers? Yes, they exist. In an intelligible context, the statement that prime numbers exist would be significant and rational. The same is obviously true of the statements that navies and public opinions exist; and if we could decide on a definition of Wednesday, either in terms of calendars or of Early Closing Days, then we could intelligibly affirm that the term so defined had in fact a practical application, so that the formula 'Wednesdays exist' would be both clear and succinct. There is no objection to using these four terms as the subject of 'exist' in one sentence provided no ambiguity results. And whether it is sensible or foolish to say that a man has a mind and a body depends on what you mean, and not on any artificial classification of words into so-called logical categories. It is evident that we may say that a man has suffered bodily injury without injury to his mind, or that he went out of his mind although his bodily health remained unimpaired. It may not be strictly true. It may be that body and mind cannot be separated any more than the nervous system can be separated from the digestive system. It is certainly impossible to draw a clear distinction between the circulatory and the digestive systems, so closely are they involved one with the other. But for numerous practical purposes such distinctions are necessary and legitimate. If there is really any objection to speaking of a man's mind, then there must be the same objection to speaking of his digestion.

Ryle is impressed with the fact that there are many words which indicate tendencies or capacities, but which cannot be used to indicate episodes or occurrences. He notes that one can, at a pinch, speak of a doctor doctoring, but not of a solicitor solicitoring; a baker can be said to bake, but a grocer "is not described as 'grocing' on any particular occasion" (p. 118). Is it really necessary to point out that such accidents of linguistic usage are without bearing on the relations between the things they are used to signify? There is no 'episodic' verb related to 'schoolmaster', yet if we call the same man a teacher we find that there is an episodic mate after all. Shall we seek some deep philosophical importance in the fact that night falls, whereas day breaks, that things may be either tasty or smelly, but not heary or seey? Some philosophers really seem to imagine that the universe must be organised after the model of their language.

Later Ryle mentions an objection to talking at all about "capacities, tendencies, liabilities and pronenesses", and says the objection is valid if such statements as "the sugar is soluble" or "the sleeper can read French" are construed as asserting "extra matters of fact" in the manner of "the old faculty theories which construed dispositional words as denoting occult agencies or causes" (pp. 119–120). In truth, the chemist, in asserting the solubility of sugar in water, is stating that there is some structural peculiarity which may or may not be fully understood, which determines the reaction of this substance in the presence of water, and which might perhaps be demonstrated without solution. Nothing 'occult' is involved. Similarly, the physiologist who asserts that a man can speak French believes that his brain has, by special training, been modified in a particular way.

Ryle then introduces us to "law sentences", and says that a hypothetical sentence is not called a law unless "the protasis can embody at least one expression like 'any' or 'whenever'." Presumably it is not a law if I say that 'If John jumps off the Monument he will be killed', but it is a law if I say that 'Any man jumping off the Monument will be killed', or 'Whenever people jump off the Monument they get killed', and so on. In other words the 'law-statement' must be general. But to distinguish the general from the singular proposition is not always easy. In the first example above the time is not specified and in that respect the proposition is general, for it is equivalent to 'Whenever John jumps . . .' But the form of words is unimportant provided the meaning is understood. What is important in either case, whether the statement is general or particular, is that all the conditions of the phenomenon in question should be known. How they are best expressed will depend on the conditions, on the person who is to make use of the information, on available methods of tabulation, and so on. Every scientific specialist devises formulas, tables, graphical expressions, and other aids to memory, exposition or record, as experience prompts and occasion permits. This 'logical' analysis of the so-called 'law-proposition' contributes nothing either to the practice or to the theory of scientific investigation, and is psychologically futile.

Ryle talks as though one could discover everything of importance about the mind by inquiring what people say, what nouns they use as complements of what verbs, what adjectives they apply to what nouns. He seems to think it an unanswerable argument if he can describe the view which he is combatting as equivalent to some grammatical oddity. Every view which a man may hold is, for him, a proposition or a grammatical expression, and its validity is determined by its conformity with a set of quasi-logical or grammatical rules which, without ever being stated clearly, are implied or suggested by quaint instances. We have to construct as best we may these fundamental rules of logic, on which everything seems to hang, from allusions to "sentences such as . . ." or "nouns like . . ." or "such verbs as . . .". Sometimes the category to which a noun belongs is 'defined' by a list of adjectives which may, in normal usage, be made to qualify it. But it is everywhere tacitly assumed that permissible conjunctions of words somehow reveal relations between things. Is it not strange that a philosopher professing such concern with the proper uses of language should be so hopelessly mistaken in his notions of what these proper uses are?

9

TRUTH AND WORDS

Martin Heidegger lived from 1889 to 1976, and George Steiner's account of him (Fontana Paperbacks, 1978) states that some commentators regard him as "a prolix charlatan and poisoner of good sense", whereas for others he is "a master of insight, a philosopher-teacher whose works may renew the inward condition of man" (p. 13). For Steiner himself, "to 'understand' Heidegger is to accept entry into an alternative order or space of meaning and of being" (p. 18).

In this chapter, Englefield studies some of Heidegger's essays included (in English translation) in Werner Brock's collection entitled Existence and Being *(London: Vision, 1949), and his page references are to this volume.*

THE EDITORS

In an essay entitled 'On the Essence of Truth', Heidegger proposes an " 'abstract' enquiry into the nature of truth, an enquiry which is bound to turn away from all reality" (p. 319). Metaphysicians frequently keep their discussions remote from reality, and I shall try to show that, in the case in question, this is to the detriment of the enquiry.

Heidegger first asks "what . . . we ordinarily understand by 'truth' ". He continues:

> What is 'something true'? We say, for example: 'It is a true pleasure to collaborate in the accomplishment of this task'. We mean, it is a pure, real joy. The True is the Real. In the same way we speak of 'true coin' as distinct from false. False coin is not really what it seems. It is only a 'seeming' and therefore unreal. The unreal stands for the opposite of the real. But counterfeit coin too is something real. Hence we say more precisely: 'real coin is genuine coin'. Yet both are 'real', the counterfeit coin in circulation no less than the genuine. Therefore the truth of the genuine coin cannot be verified by its reality. The question returns: what do 'genuine' and 'true' mean here? (p. 321)

I propose the following account of the matter: We know things by their appearance, their feel, sound, behaviour, location, and so on. But we are accustomed to recognise things long before we have had the time or opportunity to confirm the presence of *all* the characteristics which we attribute to them. In doing this, we make mistakes, supposing that we are in the presence of an object x when in fact we are dealing with z, which possesses certain characters in common with x. If an object is deliberately constructed having all the more conspicuous characters of x but no others, then we speak of it as counterfeit. When we find it necessary to discriminate between genuine and counterfeit specimens, we use the words true, genuine, real, veritable, or authentic for the former, and false, illusory, spurious, sham, deceptive, fake, bogus, fraudulent, artificial for the latter, according as we feel about it.

When Heidegger says that the counterfeit coin is also something 'real', he is using the word in another sense, where real is contrasted with imaginary. The counterfeit coin is a piece of base metal with marks on it which suggest to the superficial observer a piece of gold or silver. But an imaginary coin is not made of metal or of any other substance. In clearing up verbal ambiguities of this kind, the appropriate method is not 'to turn away from all reality', but to illustrate with concrete examples.

Heidegger turns next to the truth of propositions, and says that what is involved is "correspondence". One thing that he here seems to have in mind is that when we say that a sequence of ideas corresponds with reality, we mean that under given conditions the envisaged sequence of events would be experienced. But how about what he calls the "correspondence" of the purport of the statement with "the thing itself"? In this connection he mentions what he calls "an old, if not the oldest, tradition of thought, according to which truth is the *likeness* or *agreement* (*Übereinstimmung*; ὁμοίωσις) of a statement (λόγος) to or with a given thing (πρᾶγμα)". And this leads him to investigate "agreement". He finds that two coins may be said to agree if they are alike, but that we also speak of the agreement of the statement "the coin is round" with the thing. But, he asks, what manner of agreement is this?

> The coin is of metal. The statement is in no sense material. The coin is round. The statement has absolutely nothing spatial about it. With the coin you can buy something. The statement about it can never be legal tender. But despite the disparity between the two, the above statement agrees with and is true of the coin. (p. 326)

It is untrue to say that a statement "is in no sense material" and "has absolutely nothing spatial about it"; for it is either spoken, written, or recorded in some other manner; even if it is only thought it is a material and spatially localised brain activity. And, although statements can hardly be adapted for use as 'legal tender', it is notoriously possible to sell them. Nevertheless, it may be conceded that there is little resemblance between the sounds or letters of a statement and the facts to which it may refer. Thus, when we were considering two coins, agreement meant resemblance, but in the present instance it does not. Heidegger writes as though there were something surprising or paradoxical about this. But he must know that many common words have a variety of meanings, often so remote that no plausible connection can be traced, as in the following examples of uses of the word 'agree':

> He and his wife do not agree.
> I agreed to his proposal.
> Lobster does not agree with him.
> In French the adjective agrees with the noun.
> The two accounts do not agree.

All these are perfectly clear even without context, and it is not necessary to assume any fundamental essential meaning that underlies them all. As Mill long ago pointed out (see above, p. 83), the quest for the meaning of words, as if somewhere in Heaven this meaning were laid up, immutable and everlasting like the title-deeds of the universe, is quite vain.

This point is worth pressing, for Heidegger's discussion of 'agreement' shows that he, like many of his commentators, supposes that it is permissible to take any abstract noun and then discuss it as if it were the name of a thing, indeed of one and the same thing, whatever the context in which the word is used. Werner Brock's exposition of Heidegger's view of "the concept of 'Being' " (in the introduction to the volume from which I have been quoting) affords a striking example. This concept, he says, "is the most universal one", yet "it is obscure and indefinable" (p. 26). He goes on to speak of "the characteristics of 'Dasein' " (p. 29), meaning the characteristics of what he takes to be the thing, for he is not concerned with the characteristics of the word. He says that the term "Da-Sein" expresses its "Being". "Dasein" has a peculiar type of Being, and this is called "Existence". The fallacy here arises from a false analogy between meaning as relevant to scientific terms, and meaning as relevant to words as used in everyday contexts. If an entomologist says that bees, grasshoppers, bugs, and butterflies are all insects, he means to assert that they have certain features in common in virtue of which they merit the name, and he defines the term 'insect' by reference to these features. All scientific classification rests on the same principle. Objects or types are classed together if they possess certain characters in common, and small groups are classed together in larger groups in the same way. But such classifications are carefully constructed after exhaustive examination of the characters of all the objects concerned, and the name is not applied to a group until the common features linking its members have been ascertained and confirmed. Our common language, however, is inherited from a distant past, and the conventional association of words with things or ideas has not been scientifically established in the same way. All sorts of superficial resemblances have led to the transfer of a name from one object to another, and the existence of such a common name guarantees no common feature at all. Hence it is absurd to assume that a word which happens to be used of a number of different things represents an abstraction and denotes some kind of character or quality which is to be found in all of them.

We can construct many intelligible sentences with the

word 'be' (or with its equivalents, in its verbal conjugation). We may say 'Be off!' or 'God is', or 'I am for disarmament'. It is used with adjectives to indicate their application (he is ill, late, expected), or with adverbs and phrases (he is in the bath, through his exams). In some languages no verb at all is required in such sentences, and the order of the words suffices to indicate the complementary function of the adjective or adverb. The philosophers have not yet, as far as I know, tried to make a metaphysical entity out of word-order. But Heidegger's discussion of 'Being' is founded on making an abstract noun out of the various uses of 'is' and 'be'.

What exactly is meant by the agreement of a statement with the facts? Engineers employ gauges of various kinds to keep them informed of the conditions prevailing in the less accessible parts of a machine. These are so constructed that from the position of their pointers it is possible to infer the conditions in the engine. If such a piece of apparatus fails to register correctly, one might say that its indications did not agree with the facts. In order that such failure may be revealed, there must be alternative ways of ascertaining the facts. Thus if, when the steam gauge registers subnormal pressure, the boiler explodes, one infers that the gauge was defective. The normal agreement of the gauge-readings with the internal conditions is due to the fact that the gauge was constructed for that purpose; and the relation of correspondence between pointer position and internal pressure is established quite arbitrarily according to convenience. No one supposes that there is any resemblance in colour, shape, taste or smell between the dial and the bowels of the machine. One may establish a correspondence between any two sets of distinguishable objects. A set of names may correspond to a set of people, a set of numbers to a set of motor-cars. There is no need for the names to have the same characters as the people, or for the numbers to have any deep Pythagorean significance in relation to the cars. The notion that words must have some hidden relation to the things they stand for is as fanciful as that the number of the houses of a street should bear some mathematical relationship to the ages of the occupants. If, then, a statement may be said to agree with the facts or correspond to the facts, it is because we have established a correspondence of this kind in constructing our language, not deliberately, of course, but through the progressive adaptation of thousands of years.

Heidegger's method is to take some formula (suggesting that it is widely accepted) which includes an ambiguous term. The ambiguity is then exploited to suggest a paradox or contradiction, and fresh material for discussion is found by investigating the meaning of other terms in the formula, or by introducing new ones which give rise to distracting associations, until the whole question is inextricably confused and the muddled reader is persuaded that truth is indeed at the bottom of a well. We can follow the process through the following stages:

1. ". . . an old, if not the oldest, tradition of thought, according to which truth is the *likeness* or *agreement* . . . of a statement to or with a given thing" (quoted on p. 96 above).

2. ". . . this agreement is supposed to be an approximation" (pp. 326–7).

3. But to approximate to the coin, "the statement would have to *become* the coin and present itself entirely in that form" (p. 327. One is prompted to ask why this is necessary. Can a man not resemble his father or brother without changing his identity and presenting himself entirely in their form?)

4. But if it were the coin, it would not be like it. The moment it succeeded in becoming the coin, "the statement, as statement, could no longer agree with the thing". And so . . .

5. "In any approximation the statement has to remain, indeed it has first to become, what it is". "How", then, "can the statement precisely by insisting on its own nature approximate to something else, to the thing?" He answers:

6. " 'Approximation' in this instance cannot mean a material likeness between two things unlike in kind. The

nature of the approximation is rather determined by the kind of relationship obtaining between statement and thing'' (p. 327).

But presumably it *is* that relationship. The question 'how can the statement approximate to the thing?' is a question about the meaning of 'approximate'. And it is equivalent to: what is the relationship between statement and thing?

The state of the argument is now that truth is defined as the approximation of a statement to a thing, although we do not know what 'approximation' means. Nothing could be much more vain than to take an unclear definition and try to find some meaning for its terms that would make it acceptable. If, besides the word 'truth', there is a thing or relationship to which the word applies, then we may of course enquire further about the characteristics of this thing. But first we must know what the thing is. If you tell me that 'Ornithorhynchus' is the name of an animal found in Australasia, my knowledge is not much increased until you show me the animal or pictures of it, or describe it by comparison with other animals which I have seen. In the case of the word 'truth' you must show me examples of it, so that I may study the thing, if there is a thing. This process of explaining an idea is not the same process as defining a word. The definition of a word can be expected to be intelligible only to one who is already acquainted with the idea or the thing the word is to stand for. When a triangle is defined as a three-sided plane figure, it is assumed that we already know what is meant by three, side, plane, and figure. It is vain to give a definition in terms which must again be defined, and so on ad absurdum.

The statement with which Heidegger has been concerned is 'the coin is round'. He continues, substituting 'representation' for 'approximation', and saying:

> The statement about the coin relates 'itself' to this thing by representing it and saying of the thing represented 'how it is', 'what it is like', in whatever respect is important at that moment. The representative statement has its say about the thing represented, stating it to be *such as* it is. This 'such-as' (*so-wie*) applies to the representation and what it represents. (The words or phrases from the original German, here

and in my other quotations, have been included by the translators in
their version).

The statement, then, says what the coin is like, says that it is
such as it is, namely round. Round is what the coin is, and
round is what the statement says it is. So that the 'such-as'
applies to the statement (the representation) and to the coin
(what it represents). There is, then, roundness in the statement; the roundness of the coin is transferred in some way to
the statement, for otherwise how could it be in the statement
as well? He adds that a statement, by representing a thing,
turns it into an object in respect of us, the subject. A thing
must of course stay where it is, "stand fast in itself . . . and
manifest itself as a constant". But as an object of our consciousness it must "come across the open towards us". This
manifestation of the thing in making a move towards us is,
then, "accomplished in the open, within the realm of the
Overt (*das Offene*)". If we ask whence is derived "the overt
character (*die Offenheit*)" of "das Offene", we learn that it
"is not initially created by the representation" (presumably
one might have been forgiven for assuming this), but "is only
entered into and taken over each time as an area of relationships (*Bezugsbereich*)". The idea seems to be that the open-
ness of the open is merely temporary, a mere 'Bezugsbereich'
which opens and closes every time the coin gets represented.

Heidegger's essay amply illustrates what may fitly be
called the lure of abstraction. To understand the question
'what is truth?' one might appropriately think of other
similar abstractions, for example:

What is health? What constitutes a healthy body or mind?

What is anger? What are the characteristics of an angry
person or animal?

What is utility? In what circumstances do we say that a
thing is useful?

What is life? What are the distinguishing features of living
animals and plants?

It is very important that, in any given case, we should know how the abstraction is to be translated into more concrete terms, as above. In the case of 'truth' there are obvious possibilities of confusion. A particular true proposition is often called 'a truth', and in this sense we speak of 'home-truths'. Truth is also used for what is true. Thus we say that a man tells the truth, which means that his statements are in accordance with fact. But philosophers have tried to find some general criterion of truth. They have looked for a way of distinguishing true propositions from false by the mere inspection of the propositions.

We are surely much more likely to establish the meaning of 'truth' if we begin by inquiring what it means in ordinary practical unpretentious everyday affairs. In that connection we may say that a proposition informs us what to expect under given circumstances. Its practical utility is to guide us in dealing with our environment. When we say that it is true, we mean that reliance on it always enables us correctly to estimate environmental changes. The idea of contradiction will help to clarify further. When two propositions are contradictory, this means that they respectively lead us to expect things or events which experience tells us do not occur together; they imply a combination of conditions which we know from experience do not occur in combination. If experience of the subject is lacking, we cannot tell whether there is a contradiction or not. The words of the propositions must be replaced by the ideas of events, things or conditions which they represent, and memory must then decide whether these things do in fact occur together. Where memory fails, we can resort to experiment. If there exist verbal forms such that they themselves betray an incompatibility between the things they represent, then the process of interpretation into concrete images may be dispensed with. But this is the case only with words which represent situations with which we are thoroughly familiar. We can all think reliably in words on certain familiar topics, but not on matters concerning which we have not already built up an adequate fund of experience. A workman, for instance, knows that he can mitre this, plane that, and join certain parts in one of several ways. In reviewing in his mind the possibilities, he may often allow a sequence of words to play the part of a more representative imagery. Whether he can do so without being led astray will depend on whether he has learned to match the verbal formulas consistently with his manipulative acts. The amateur, at least, will often find that his verbal combinations are deceptive. He says to himself that he will first join the sides and then fasten the hinges, and so on. But when he comes to carry out the plan thus sketched merely in words, he finds that he had 'forgotten' that it would be impossible to use a screwdriver when the parts had been already assembled. In fact he had not forgotten it, but had never realised it. Each of the familiar separate operations could be expressed by a verbal formula, and in his mind he had put these formulas together in what seemed a suitable order, unable to see in the verbal forms the real operations which could not possibly be performed in that order.

In another essay, entitled 'Hölderlin and the Essence of Poetry', Heidegger writes: "The affirmation of human existence, and hence its essential consummation, occurs through freedom of decision" (p. 298). It is difficult to understand the 'hence'. Is human existence 'consummated' through being affirmed or because it has been affirmed? And how are we to understand human existence being affirmed through freedom of decision? Perhaps he means that if man had not been endowed with free will he could not have affirmed his existence and so consummated it. But how can he know what man could have accomplished under such limitations? The argument proceeds: "This freedom lays hold of the necessary and places itself in the bonds of a supreme obligation". He might mean that man, being free, decides to resign his freedom by submitting to a self-imposed law. But this would be to confound two kinds of freedom, indeterminism and absence of social or moral constraint. One cannot, of course, justly complain of the ambiguity of a sentence considered in isolation. But hardly any sentence in the paragraph from which I have been quoting bears any obvious relation to context. It will be noticed that the difficulty of understanding this kind of writing is not due to the use of technical terms. All the words and phraseology are common and familiar.

In an essay called 'What is Metaphysics?' Heidegger mentions Hegel's well-known dictum that philosophy, seen from the point of view of sound common sense, is the world stood on its head (p. 355). This was intended by Hegel to show his contempt for common sense, and is mentioned by Heidegger in the same spirit. In his essay 'On the Essence of Truth' he disparages "sound common sense" on the ground that it "inveighs against all knowledge of the nature of 'what-is'—that essential knowledge which has long been called 'Philosophy' " (p. 320). What common sense seems like to such a philosopher one may imagine. But unfortunately the conventions of our language are rather bound up with those of common sense. Hence philosophers who despise the latter are at a great disadvantage in using the same language that other people use for more vulgar purposes. It would be better if they could invent a new language, free from all the disturbing associations of science and sense, adapted exclusively for the approximation and manifestation of such-as and how-is-it. They could then utter the wisdom that is in them without the need to torture and disfigure our common language, which we need to keep clean and efficient for practical use.

What must surely be clear from all this is the sheer incoherence of Heidegger's writings. If he were a unique aberration, he would not be worth attention; but he is in many respects typical of a school of German metaphysicians which has flourished since the end of the eighteenth century. During the nineteenth century the disease spread to Britain and elsewhere, with the cult of Immanuel Kant, of which I have written in another chapter. What is deplorable is that young students, hoping no doubt to acquire wisdom by studying philosophy, should be fed on such rubbish. One of two effects may be expected from the treatment: either they realise that they do not understand a word and suffer discouragement and self-distrust, or they fail to realise it, and their minds are stuffed with jargon and make-believe, with which they see nothing amiss. Some of them then discover that they can without much difficulty write the same kind of stuff themselves and win applause for it, and so it perpetuates itself.

10

CONCLUSIONS

The subjects which mostly excite the curiosity of reflective people tend to be those which have been drawn most recently into the domain of scientific enquiry, namely the problems of health and sickness, social and political organisation, and the nature, origins, and destiny of man and the universe around him. These are the subjects in which primitive ideas tend to persist, and in which the influence of religious authority has lasted longest.

This persistence of primitive ideas has to be borne in mind if we are to understand the history of modern philosophy. In this field sheer disinterested curiosity has often played only a minor role. Without the incentive of a belief to defend it is doubtful whether there could have been any speculation at all on some of the questions which in fact have attracted attention. Even when practical questions have been raised the answers have only too often been affected by emotional preference for one solution rather than another. It might almost be said that the history of modern philosophy is the history of man's endeavour to find excuses for believing what he wants to believe. The problems which are commonly held to be the most refractory will often be found to be difficult only for those who are determined to justify a preconceived solution.

Apart from the tendency to direct one's arguments towards a desired conclusion, the chief defect of most metaphysical writing is confusion arising from the use of abstractions. The abridgements of practical thought are so familiar, and reliance on verbalised processes in thinking about practical affairs is so continually justified, that the danger of relying on words where more general ideas are involved is easily overlooked. So long as familiar concrete things only are involved, the words at once evoke a clear idea of the operation referred to, and the succeeding thought processes are based on such ideas and not on the verbal formula. But when the ideas are more general and abstract, the number of possible relations between them becomes much greater, and much less easily imagined in visual or auditory or tactile terms. Then it is that the thought processes, instead of being based on the more or less reliable memory of real things and experienced events, depend more and more on verbal analogies, and analogous verbal forms are tacitly taken to represent analogous processes in the real world.

Such normal mental processes as generalisation, abstraction, analogy, and hypothesis, which are essential to all effective thought, are, in more reflective minds, subject to abuses that occur less readily in minds closely and continuously occupied with practical affairs. We see this as much in ancient or savage thought as in modern philosophers. The records of early human activity imply both the practical struggle to tame the environment and the imaginative overflow which appears as soon as there is a respite from the struggle. So long as the problems raised were practical and urgent, any solutions proposed would be quickly tested, and adopted or discarded according to results. But in times of leisure and comparative prosperity men could afford the luxury of uncontrolled speculation. For the solution of speculative problems they had, however, no other resources but the ideas and methods which had served them in the practical field. Accordingly it is to this practical knowledge that we have to trace, not only the magical and religious notions of the savage, but also the speculations of more recent times.

If the relation between language and thought had been understood, there might have been less of that kind of literature which flourishes on the assumption that where two or three words are gathered together, there is bound to be a meaning associated with them; although a better understanding of the matter might not much have affected common practice. If some forms of literature consist of almost pure verbiage, this is probably due less to the ignorance of writers than to the pleasure which they derive from uninhibited utterance, and to the gratification which they are conscious of affording to many earnest people who are more eager to be edified than to understand. There are other products of civilisation besides literary verbiage which are more popular than wholesome, and we cannot expect the purveyor of such products to be more sensitive to the true interests of his customers than they are themselves.

Although much of the pleasure derived from the purveyance and consumption of meaningless writing may be comparatively innocent, there is a tendency for the commodity to spread to fields where it is less harmless. The vain theorising of the metaphysician, the incoherence of the poet and the literary theorist, the effusions of the music and art critics, may be reckoned a form of indulgence more ridiculous than hurtful. But when this make-believe appears in writings on psychology, sociology, ethics, education, and politics it is a more serious matter. And it seems as if the habit of sham reasoning, practised at first in the service of literature or philosophy, easily passes over into every other domain of thought which is not protected by the necessity for continuous practical application. Our present system of education allows many young persons to be brought up on a regime in which the main stress is laid on the so-called humanities, and this means especially literature. It is just here that the vicious practice of permitting words to masquerade as ideas is most common. Students are encouraged to write appraisals of poetry which they cannot even be expected to understand, and are then commended for composing sonorous phrases and using cant words. If they do not come to despise the whole business and perhaps acquire a contemptuous attitude to all literature, they can hardly help being infected by this training, so that they try to employ the same methods in writing and thinking on other topics.

The universities, with their distinct 'faculties' of arts and science, encourage the view that there are two kinds of subject, that the methods appropriate to the two cases are quite different, and even that there exist two distinct types of mind, the scientific and the academic, the one adapted to material things and the other to the concerns of 'culture'. If it is usual nowadays to stress the need of a balanced education, that is to say of giving the science student some smattering of culture and the arts student some smattering of science, this is only because the two studies are held to be different in kind and to require the application of distinct faculties in the mind, each of which has to be appropriately exercised.

Of course every branch of science has its special methods, indeed every specific problem is solved only by a method appropriate to it. It is therefore obvious that the procedures of the chemist, biologist, physiologist, astronomer, and geologist must all be different, though for particular purposes they borrow from one another. There is no fundamental distinction that separates the anthropological from the physical sciences. Observation, experiment, use of models— these are the essential methods of all endeavours to study nature, whether animate or inanimate, on the molecular or the social level. The unity of science is also apparent from the fact that every investigator turns at need to his colleagues in other fields and borrows their knowledge or methods. This is just as true of history, archeology, sociology, and psychology as of biology or chemistry.

NOTES

EDITORS' INTRODUCTION

1. J. M. Guyau, *Esquisse d'une morale sans obligation ni sanction*, 11th edn., Paris: Alcan, 1909; *L'irréligion de l'avenir*, 23rd edn., Paris: Alcan, 1927.

2. Robertson's arguments in *Christianity and Mythology* (second edn., 1910) and *Pagan Christs* (second edn., 1911) convinced Englefield that Jesus was a mythological rather than a historical figure; and Robertson's *Short History of Christianity* (second edn., 1913) and *History of Freethought* (1936) taught him that the history of Christianity was a deeply shameful one. (All four of these books were published at London by Watts.) A volume of essays on Robertson by several hands, entitled *J. M. Robertson (1856–1933): Liberal, Rationalist and Scholar*, was published by Pemberton (London) in 1987.

CHAPTER 1: THE HAZARDS OF FINE WRITING

1. John Dewey, *Logic* (1938). I quote from the reprint published by Allen and Unwin in London in 1939, p. 57.

2. Joy Paul Guilford, *General Psychology*, London: Chapman and Hall, 1939, p. 234.

3. Kenneth Burke, *The Philosophy of Literary Form, Studies in Symbolic Action*, 3rd edn., Berkeley/Los Angeles/London: Louisiana State University Press, 1973, pp. 4–6.

4. T. S. Eliot, *Selected Essays*, 3rd edn., London: Faber and Faber, 1951, p. 406.

5. A. Schopenhauer, 'Über Schriftstellerei und Stil', in *Werke*, ed. M. Brasch, 7th edn., Leipzig: G. Fock, n.d., vol. ii, p. 688.

6. Schopenhauer, preface to first edn. of *Die beiden Grundprobleme der Ethik*, 1840.

CHAPTER 2: VICES OF LITERARY CRITICISM

1. T. Carlyle, *On Heroes, Hero-Worship and the Heroic in History*, London: Chapman and Hall, 1907, pp. 155ff (Lecture 5).

2. W. Wordsworth, 'Poetry and Poetic Diction' (Preface to the 2nd edn. of *Lyrical Ballads*, 1800), in *English Critical Essays (Nineteenth Century)*, ed. E. D. Jones, London: Oxford University Press, 1947 (in the series *The World's Classics*), p. 16.

3. P. B. Shelley, 'A Defence of Poetry' (1821), in *Ibid.*, pp. 109, 130, 131.

4. F. R. H. Englefield, 'The Origin, Functions and Development of Poetry', *Trivium*, 10 (1975), pp. 62–73. [The substance of this article is also included in Englefield's book *The Mind at Work and Play*, Buffalo: Prometheus, 1985, ch. 14. Eds.].

5. I. A. Richards, *Principles of Literary Criticism*, 3rd edn., London: Kegan Paul, 1944, pp. 32–33.

6. I. A. Richards, *Practical Criticism*, London: Kegan Paul, 1929, p. 261.

7. *Op. cit.* in note 5 above, p. 62.

8. F. R. Leavis, *New Bearings in English Poetry*, new edn. London: Chatto and Windus, 1950, pp. 77–78.

CHAPTER 3: THE USES OF 'INTUITION'

1. "God", says Leibniz in his *A New System of Nature* (1695), "created the soul, or every other real unity, in the first place in such a way that everything with it comes into existence from its own

substance through perfect spontaneity as regards itself, and in perfect harmony with objects outside itself" (*Philosophical Works*, edited by G. M. Duncan, New Haven: Tuttle, Morehouse and Taylor, 1890, p. 77).

CHAPTER 4: KANT AS DEFENDER OF THE FAITH

1. Quoted in J. L. May, *The Oxford Movement*, London: John Lane, 1933, pp. 105–06.

2. T. de Quincey, 'Rhetoric', in *Collected Writings*, vol. x, London, 1897, p. 122–23.

3. Quoted in J. A. Froude's *Carlyle. The First Forty Years*, vol. i, London: Longmans, Green & Co., 1882, p. 196.

4. *Ibid.*, p. 361.

5. Carlyle, *Critical and Miscellaneous Essays*, London: Chapman and Hall, 1894, vol. i, p. 63.

6. For full details of Coleridge's and Carlyle's references, see R. Wellek, *Immanuel Kant in England, 1798–1838*, Princeton: Princeton University Press, 1931.

7. J. S. Mill, *Autobiography*, London: Longmans, Green: 1873, pp. 272–73.

8. *Ibid.*, pp. 273–74.

9. J. H. Stirling, *The Secret of Hegel*, London: Longman, Green, 1865, vol. i.

10. Quoted in G. O. Trevelyan, *Life and Letters of Lord Macaulay*, London: Longmans, 1908, p. 515.

CHAPTER 6: THE NEW THEOLOGY

1. J. A. T. Robinson, *Honest to God*, London: SCM, 1963, p. 47. Further references to this book will be given as page references in the text of my chapter.

2. J. S. Bezzant, 'Intellectual Objections', in *Objections to*

Christian Belief, with an introduction by A. R. Vidler, London: Constable, 1963, p. 106.

CHAPTER 7: THINGS, IDEAS, AND WORDS

1. Descartes, *Les principes de la philosophie*, part 1, no. 74.

2. Henry Hallam, *Introduction to the Literature of Europe in the Fifteenth, Sixteenth and Seventeenth Centuries*, 4-vol. edn., vol. iii, London: John Murray, 1882, p. 81.

3. C. S. Sherrington, *Integrative Action of the Nervous System*, new edn., Cambridge: Cambridge University Press, 1947, p. 286.

4. Leibniz, 'Thoughts on Knowledge, Truth and Ideas', from the Latin: *Acta Eruditorum Lipsiensium* (1684); in *Philosophical Works*, as cited in note 1 to ch. 3 above, pp. 28–29.

5. Hume, *A Treatise of Human Nature* (1739), part 1, section 7.

6. The following account, from here to the end of this chapter, is that given by Englefield in his *Language: Its Origin and Its Relation to Thought*, London: Elek/Pemberton, and New York: Scribner, 1977, pp. 137–39.

7. Goethe, *Faust*, part 1, line 1996 ('that is just where a word puts in a timely appearance').

8. Note by John Stuart Mill in James Mill's *Analysis of the Phenomena of the Human Mind*, edited with notes by J. S. Mill, London: Longmans Green, 1869, vol. i, pp. 236–37.

9. Kant says, for instance: "General logic . . . makes abstraction of all content of cognition, that is, of all relation of cognition to its object, and regards only the logical form in the relation of cognitions to each other, that is, the form of thought in general" (*Critique of Pure Reason*, English translation by J. Meiklejohn, Everyman edition, London: Dent, 1934, p. 65). But we do not know what the 'logical form' is. It would be equally possible to say that we must abstract from a tablecloth its size, material, shape,

colour, and use, and that there would then remain the 'general tablecloth' or some other X.

CHAPTER 8: 'CATEGORY MISTAKES'

1. Bertrand Russell, *Human Knowledge*, London: Allen and Unwin, 1948, pp. 213–14. Italics mine.

INDEX